A Loving God
God

& a Suffering
World

A New Look at an Old Problem

Jon Tal Murphree

InterVarsity Press
Downers Grove
Illinois 60515

InterVarsity Press is the book-publishing division of Inter-Varsity Christian Fellowship, a student movement active on campus at hundreds of universities, colleges and schools of nursing. For information about local and regional activities, write IVCF, 233 Langdon St., Madison, WI 53703.

Distributed in Canada through InterVarsity Press, 1875 Leslie St., Unit 10, Don Mills, Ontario M3B 2M5, Canada.

All Scripture quotations, unless otherwise indicated, are from the Revised Standard Version of the Bible, copyrighted 1946, 1952, © 1971, 1973.

Cover illustration: Marcus Hamilton

ISBN 0-87784-877-7

Printed in the United States of America

Library of Congress Cataloging in Publication Data

Murphree, Jon Tal.
    A loving God and a suffering world.

    Includes bibliographical references.
        1. God–Omnipotence.   2. God–Goodness.
3. Providence and government of God.   4. Good and
evil.   5. Suffering–Moral and religious aspects.
I. Title.
BT133.M87   231   81-11759
ISBN 0-87784-877-7   AACR2

18	17	16	15	14	13	12	11	10	9	8	7	6	5	4	3	2	1
95	94	93	92	91	90	89	88	87	86	85	84	83	82	81			

*to
our two-year-old
Mark
the lovingest little nuisance
any author ever had*

Introduction

When dealing with the evil of suffering we have a double problem. First, something acceptable to the intellect needs to be said to help us understand some of the reasons for pain. Second, something emotionally satisfying needs to be said to help us bear the pain. Both are serious and difficult problems.

For me the second is more difficult than the first. Without minimizing the intellectual problem, I can nevertheless accept suffering intellectually more easily than I can bear it emotionally. I am still horrified by the memory of nightmares I had as a child. I have lost hours of sleep sympathizing with Hansel and Gretel and even with the wicked witch who ended up in the oven. Preparing this manuscript has made me sick to my stomach. I have had to fight off depression as I reflected on the problem. Were it not for the grace of God I would have succumbed a long time ago to my fatalistic, pessimistic propensities. I personally need fortitude more than I need explanations.

Since pain is a matter of feeling, however, there are those for whom an explanation must be emotionally satisfying before it can be intellectually acceptable. Suffering must be justified to the emotions; otherwise it cannot be justified to the mind. Because hurting affects the emotions, no explanation will even be considered until the hurting ends. The very existence of pain allows for no justification.

It may be a confession of weakness on my part, but I need an intellectual explanation to help me handle suffering emotionally. My emotions need all the help they can get. When there is nothing either intellectually or emotionally to hang on to, suffering is devastating.

Because of my weakness and cowardice, I have disqualified myself from saying much about bearing pain. In this volume I am speaking more to the mind than to the emotions. The project has been attempted cautiously, realizing the dangers of idle philosophizing and the liability of writing while aloof from the harsh brutal input of pain itself. On the other hand, it is probably easier to think discriminately while we are not in the emotional quasi-trauma of bearing pain. It is even more difficult to think rationally while we are contemplating the suffering of those dearest to us.

So it is my purpose, first, to help those who with open minds wish to consider the Christian position, and second, to aid believers who seek honestly acceptable reasons on which they can "pin the blame" for evil.

1
WHAT
THE
PROBLEM
IS NOT

AFTER I HAD GIVEN AN ADDRESS to a junior-college student body in Kentucky, a male student stroked his beard with an unmistakable academic air and asked, "So you postulate the existence of God and then set out to find evidence to support it?"

For a moment I felt the frustration of being grossly misunderstood, inferring from his question that my lecture had been ambiguous and misleading. Of course I moved quickly to eliminate that feeling by choosing to believe that the student had been inattentive.

"Quite the contrary," I replied. "What I said is that one begins with the evidence and allows the evidence to speak for itself. To some of us the evidence for God is so convincing and so conclusive that we cannot deny it without insulting our own intelligence."

My answer was not intended as a putdown nor was it taken as such. Though some of us think that intellectual honesty compels *us* to believe, we do not consider the basis of our belief a reflection on either the intelligence or the honesty of anyone attempting with an open mind to sift through what seems to be conflicting evidence.

There Is Evil . . .
The presence of evil in a universe alleged to have been built and ordered by a God who is both good and infinitely powerful poses a difficult problem to anyone wishing to take seriously the Christian claims. No living creature, human or animal, has escaped the common lot of suffering. Disease, accidents, earthquakes and other natural calamities, emotional stress, even mental pain—these are real and ruthless. Evil is returned for good; sacrifice results in suffering; the innocent absorb fallout from cruel acts of guilty individuals who apparently go on without retribution. Accidents are senseless and absurd, without rhyme or reason. Life is a bundle of contradictions, with ludicrous and incongruent stupidities.

"Why me, God?" Inquisitive minds through the centuries have attempted to sort out the puzzle. "I have tried to be good and do what's right. And then, this!" At times life seems to be nothing more than a big fat question mark.

Evil is taken as evidence against the kind of God the Christian theologian defends. The problem is overlooked only by those Christians who are more committed to their own tradition with its accompanying emotional security than they are to honesty in their search for truth. Other Christians admit that, on the surface at least, there appears to be a real problem. But even if the existence of evil in the world should constitute serious evidence against God, it should in all fairness be weighed against what some of us are convinced is a preponderance of evidence supporting the Christian God.

... But There Is Good

It is ironic almost to the point of comedy that people should so focus on evil that they blindly overlook the immeasurable abundance of good, happiness, even pleasure carried by this planet at every given point in time. Should we count the thorns without counting the stars? Do we forget that there is more peace than war and more beauty than ugliness? Why should we focus on hate and miss seeing love, or hear the groans of grief but be deaf to the songs of joy? There are lights in the world as well as shadows. There is virtue as well as vice. Our senses provide us with more pleasure than pain. On any fair estimate, the sheer volume of beauty, pleasure, goodness and happiness in the world would eclipse the very highest count of evil.

Though it is not expressed and is generally unrecognized, I have picked up vibrations of a vague feeling among many nontheists that the world somehow is "supposed" to be good. If you ask them, they will surely say it is supposed to be good only if there is a good God. But the idea keeps coming through that the world should be good, God or no God. Goodness is expected to be the norm. The Christian God sometimes seems to be a scapegoat for the rancor produced when the expected good is not experienced.

This expectation of good might be derived either from an unquenchable desire to see goodness in the world or from a culture that expects goodness because of the influence of the Christian notion that God is good. I suspect, however, that goodness has become the norm because there is so much of it in the world.

If there is a feeling that the world should be good, as I have surmised, I am wondering whether there is any valid reason why it is "supposed" to be good other than the assumption of a good God. Do we not sort of nebulously presuppose such a good God by assuming that the world should be good?

The fact that pain and evil so catch our attention probably means that they are the exception and that goodness and happiness *are* in fact the rule. Perhaps the reason we focus on pain is that it is seen to be such a contrast to the norm. In music a discord is glaring precisely because we are accustomed to harmony. A few glaring faults in a public speaker stand out because he or she otherwise has given a smooth presentation. The number of fumbles is listed in the "stats" of a football game simply because fumbles are not regularly made. Discord does not belong to a composition; speaking defects do not belong to a speech; fumbles are exceptions in a game. How could we ever discover ugliness except in contrast to beauty? How could we detect disorder except as an irregularity in a world that regularly functions in an orderly way? When we deal with evil we are dealing with something like an alien ingredient that seems out of place in a world normally ordered by goodness.

Certainly, we wish to explain evil as far as possible, but the explanation we give must also as far as possible explain beauty, harmony and virtuous deeds. The good has to be accounted for as well as the bad. And that, I am suggesting, is what nontheists are not in a position to do. By virtue of their nontheistic position, they generally assume that they themselves are the product of nonrational causes; yet can they really believe that such nonrational causes could produce the rational mind they discover in themselves, with its capacity to appreciate beauty, truth and virtue? It is a logical contradiction to expect a cause to produce an effect not even the seeds of which can be contained in the cause. Can a moronic universe produce rational intelligence? That kind of groundless faith is surely under a heavier strain to authenticate than even the most naive Christian faith. Nontheists require more credulity for their position than do theists.

A premed student had professed a Christian faith

throughout his first three years at the university. Sometime before his graduation, Clifford said to me, "I have chucked the whole thing about God. There are simply too many intellectual problems the Christian faith cannot answer."

After a period of open dialog, I inquired, "Tell me, Cliff, has your new position resolved your problems?"

He replied, "Heavens, no! It has raised more questions than it has settled."

The Problem of Good

Certainly the evidence supporting the Christian view only begins with good, order and purposiveness in the world—like the footprints of God in the sand of this island planet. But if we are going to talk about evil, disorder and meaninglessness, something needs to be said for those other more abundant characteristics. If we cannot explain the shadows and be consistent with our view of a good God, we also cannot explain the light and be consistent with rejection of the goodness of God. The case we make for God should not stand or fall on how we answer nontheists on the "problem of evil"—without a consideration of the way they answer theists on the "problem of good."

What has been called the "problem of evil" is really no problem at all for an atheist who keeps God off the scene; it is a problem only for Christian claims that assert the goodness of God. The atheist is confronted with the formidable problem of good that fits nowhere into a system that excludes God altogether.[1] A teen-age girl said to me, "There's simply got to be a God. What I see in the world does not fit together without it."

I heard a prominent atheist remark, "Don't ask me why there is order in the universe. I tell you I do not know. I only know God could not be responsible for it." Just as the problem of evil can be brushed aside by thoughtless Christians, the much larger problem of good can be brushed aside by thoughtless non-Christians.

Indeed, some of us wonder whether the problem of evil has not been pounced on like a carcass and picked to the bones while the problem of good has gone almost unnoticed. We wonder whether the evil problem may be philosophically popular simply because it is one of the few things skeptics feel they can get a handle on.

Christian faith should be based on *evidence for* weighed against *evidence against*. Unless the alleged fact of God is regarded as intrinsically improbable, the evidence *for* God is overwhelming if considered with an open mind. The Christian thinks that the evidence *against* is so overbalanced by evidence *for* that a denial—or even a skeptical position of doubt—is more irrational than belief. There is no reason to think that all the problems have to be explained away before one acts on the evidence.

In this book I am welcoming the challenge of the problem of evil, simply because I believe that Christian assertions regarding God are truth claims that are subject to intellectually honest scrutiny. I am not suggesting, however, that those claims require rational proof—only that they require adequate and acceptable evidence, part of which we find in the existence of good.

But since I am dealing with the problem of evil rather than the problem of good, I am not attempting a defense for the existence of God. I do not consider God to be on trial. Certainly he does not need someone like me to go to bat for him. He is not about to be stripped of his eternal majesty and glory. Simply because he *is* God, he needs no exoneration for whatever he does. The "ways of God" do not need justifying to human beings as much as the "ways of man" need justifying to God.

The problem of this book is not the existence of God, but the existence of evil. I will be considering the existence of God only insofar as it is included in the problem of evil, without treating the problem of good which figures more largely into any consideration of the existence of God. Whether I am able to justify the existence of evil says very little about the nontheist's problem with the existence of good. The case for the existence of God rests more with his problem than with mine.

2
FORMULATING
THE
PROBLEM

THE QUESTION OF EVIL is hardly an imaginative inquiry. It is a profound problem, but it takes very little creativity to formulate. Considered by Augustine, Aquinas and Hume, it has been articulated more specifically by John Stuart Mill and used against the theistic position by J. L. Mackie and other modern philosophers.

Simply stated, the question is this: If God is good and if he is all-powerful, why is there evil in the world? It becomes a logical problem when stated like this: If God is good he would want to eliminate evil and if he is omnipotent he can do whatever he wishes, yet there is evil in the world. Therefore God is either not omnipotent or he is not good. That accusation strikes at the heart of the theistic position.

If any two of the three propositions are true, it is contended that the third will necessarily be false. If God is both good and all-powerful, evil would not exist. If God is good and evil exists, then he is not all-powerful. If he is all-powerful and evil exists, then he cannot be good.

Historical Answers

Some religions like Christian Science have attempted to avoid the problem altogether by denying the real existence of pain. Others have focused their attention on overcoming the reality of suffering. Gautama the Buddha located the cause of pain in human desire and shifted his emphasis to eliminating the suffering by ceasing to desire.

Others have attacked the problem by compromising divine omnipotence. The Manichaean principle, thoroughly rejected as a heresy by the Christian church as early as the sixteenth century, taught a basic dualism in the universe consisting of both good and evil. Our souls were made by the good principle and our bodies by the evil. Manichaeism recognized both the existence of evil and the goodness of God, but it compromised his omnipotence.

Other views modify the omnipotence of God by accounting for evil by logical necessity. To Leibnitz, this world with its evil is the best of all possible worlds. To others, evil is seen as a necessary stage of God's project which will ultimately be brought to perfection. Eastern Orthodoxy holds such a theodicy of development, and scholars of modern theology like Schleiermacher and popular preachers like Leslie Weatherhead have insisted that certain evil is necessary for such virtues as sympathy, compassion and heroism. Similarly, though without the Christian hope for future perfection, a theodicy of process based on Whitehead has compromised divine omnipotence by placing God within the system of "becoming" rather than being the perfection outside the system toward which all development moves. American Personal Idealism has accounted for the evil side of life by a finite God who is struggling to achieve goodness in the world.

Nietzsche's Zarathustra, on the other hand, compromised the goodness of God by having him the creator of both good and evil systems. He was the god of falsehood as well as truth, pain as well as pleasure. Not to be identified with Zoroastrianism, Islam nevertheless teaches that pain is in the purposes of Allah. That view is held while at the same time asserting that God is merciful and compassionate. To some that would be contradictory and would violate the kind of goodness many attribute to God. Similarly, some of the older, more undisciplined proponents of Calvinism held God to be the efficient cause or author of sin.

The view that is held more generally by Christians today sees moral evil resulting from the abuse of free will. Natural evil is accounted for in two ways. First, there is an evil personality (devil), not equal to God but allowed by God to have certain privileges with humanity. Second, God allows the evil both as punishment for sin and for testing Christian character. In order to prevent compromising God's omnipotence, this view has to hold that God does have the power to prevent whatever he is willing to allow. And so as not to reflect on his goodness, a distinction is made between God's perfect will for human beings and his permissive will.

The Approach of This Book
My answer to this troublesome question is a traditional Christian yes to all three of the propositions: God is good; he is omnipotent; evil does exist. The propositions of God's goodness and his omnipotence are compatible with a recognition of the existence of evil in such a way that the existence of evil does not invalidate either of the other propositions. I am convinced that the three are reconcilable in a way that does no injustice to any one of them.

My approach includes a combination of certain elements in both the free-will approach and the necessity theory, avoiding—I hope—the booby traps ordinarily associated with those approaches. The problem will be discussed in the context of what I consider to be appropriate meanings to attach to the terms *omnipotence, goodness* and *evil.* Proper definition is crucial because the terms have often been defined so loosely that the concepts become vague and almost meaningless, with little substance for us to deal with. I do not consider my definitions to be modifications of what the terms should appropriately mean. Rather they are intended to concentrate and solidify the meanings into something substantive. The word *definition* itself includes clarifying not only what something means but also what it does not mean. Without restricting definitions each term can mean almost anything anyone wishes it to mean—omnipotence can include magic and analytical absurdities; goodness can mean softness and sentimentality; evil can include anything that is vaguely inconvenient.

The definitions I give will allow each concept to interact with additional ingredients that may either compound the problem or figure into its solution. My definitions will allow omnipotence, goodness and evil to be affected by other propositions that may be asserted and agreed on. "Omnipotence" will then be in a position to react to the notion of absurdity rather than simply to swallow it up. "Goodness" will allow the sacrifice of a lesser good for the sake of a greater good without becoming less than goodness.

The alleged contradiction of the three propositions is ordinarily based on the assumption that there are no additional premises. Alvin Plantinga has a point that these propositions alone are not contradictory, and his point prevents the existence of evil from violating the notion of a good, omnipotent God.[2] The propositions are not contradictory because they leave room for all sorts of additional premises that do no violence to the ones stated.

To say that if God were both good and all-powerful he would eliminate evil is to assume that it is impossible for God to have a reason to allow evil to run its course, or a reason *not* to operate for the time being from omnipotence; or that it is impossible for him to have a greater goodness in mind than our limited vision of goodness. Often overlooked are those elements of divine justice, truth, wisdom and omniscience which in certain situations could affect the logic of the conclusion. We may be safe in saying that the combination of omnipotence with goodness would eliminate evil *provided* there are no additional ingredients, no extenuating elements, no contingent imponderables, no possible variables. God would immediately eliminate all evil *provided* there are no overriding conditions to prevent it. But as soon as we define our terms so that we understand what they do not mean, then we recognize that certain conditions could possibly prevail that would violate the proviso of those definitions. In order to be credible, the argument of contradictory propositions requires an additional premise that rules out all contingencies, a premise that limits the argument to the propositions stated. This we do not have.

Our Limited Knowledge

Some of the variables that we think we know I will discuss in later chapters. But I am not suggesting that I know all of them. For this reason I shall never have all the answers to the problem of evil. If I should know every reason God has in mind for allowing evil to continue for a period, then I suppose my knowledge would approach omniscience. What kind of God would he be if all his ways and reasons could be understood by such an insignificant creature as I? The prophet Isaiah quoted God as saying, "For my thoughts are not your thoughts, neither are your ways my ways. . . . For as the heavens are higher than the earth, so are my ways higher than your ways and my thoughts than your thoughts" (Is 55:8-9).

If God should be up to anything like what is claimed by Christians—and if God is indeed God—then we would expect him to be up to something beyond our ability to comprehend fully. That expectation does not ride on the distinction between rational mind and nonrational (for we consider ourselves to have a measure of rationality), but rather on the difference between infinite mind and finite mind. We would expect God to have some reasons that transcend human understanding. Don't you suppose my dog thought I was terribly inconsiderate when I hushed him late one night, or unmercifully cruel when I refused to let him eat the dumplings he had smelled? He had no idea that his barking was keeping my neighbors awake, or that small pieces of broken glass had fallen into the food. The dog's ignorance at that point does not necessarily reflect irrationality on his part. He was simply *not in a position* to grasp my reasons. My reasons transcended his understanding.

Attempts to reveal to a finite mind all the purposes being incubated in an infinite mind would be futile on God's part. The Christian system has never taught that God's revelation is exhaustive. Why should it be? If it can be an adequate guide for faith and conduct without being exhaustive, as is claimed, that is sufficient.

Christians should never feel smug with tidy answers to complex problems, because all the evidence is not in and all causes and reasons are not available to us. There is mystery even in God's love that commands reverence and worship. An element of mystery at the heart of reality calls for respect, awe and humility. We are not in a position to know all the answers. An honest recognition of our limited access to all possible variables should make both theist and nontheist enter into dialog with profound humility. Because of the darkness we must always be modest. But the darkness which we recognize should never blind us to the light that is obvious. Accepting our ignorance with modesty, we should never sanctify it as a virtue. A high premium has been placed on ignorance by some naive Christians as a means of justifying their faith. But certain skeptics have also valued ignorance as a means of justifying their doubt. Reality must be scrutinized with disciplined curiosity to understand as much as we can. Our understanding includes the realization that God may have reasons we have never discovered, reasons that would add ingredients to the logic. And God's reasons, if we could know them, would add evidence to the theistic position justifying the existence of evil.

There is no virtue in suspending judgment in the face of overwhelming evidence stacking up on one side. As we act on information we do have and on insights we gain, some important conclusions about God should be reached, however tentative they may be.

3
WHAT OMNIPOTENCE MEANS

THE CYNIC ASKED, "SO your God is able to do anything, huh?" And the unthinking Christian replied, "Certainly!" To which the questioner retorted, "Can he create a stone too big for him to lift? Is he able to make a snowball so heavy that he cannot roll it?"

That trick question is so old it has whiskers. It is intended to show that God cannot be all-powerful. If the answer to the query is yes, then God cannot throw the stone he has created, which means he is not omnipotent. If the answer is no, then he is unable to do at least one thing, and that inability shows he is not all-powerful—even though the one thing he cannot do is to limit his own power. Heads, God loses; tails, God loses.

The assumption of the question is based on a confusion,

recognition of which will help me define the term *omnipotence*. The confusion lies in what is meant by the word *power* and what is meant by the word *ability*. God's omnipotence is impugned only by collapse of a distinction between what the subject contains in itself and how it stands in relation to its object. Power is something like a strength or energy contained in the subject—whether or not an object is capable of being affected by that power. Ability, on the other hand, is never understood apart from an object; it is ability *to do* a certain thing, *to accomplish* a certain task. For a subject to have an ability to do, the object must have an "ability" to be done; that is, it must be capable of being affected by the subject.

We may justifiably broaden the definition of power as is popularly done to include such qualities as skill and authority. Even with the broader definition, however, power is understood more in terms of what a being is within itself rather than in its capacity to affect an object. Stripped of its extra baggage, power does not mean ability at all.

Since for certain tasks, ability requires power to be able to affect the object, ability is therefore a broader, more inclusive term. For other tasks, ability does not require power in the least—it requires a certain character, personality patterns or special relationships. It seems obvious that accomplishing certain tasks is not at all a matter of power. One can add strength or skill or authority *ad infinitum* and never come any nearer accomplishing a task that cannot be done. The power may be infinite while the ability is nil. Some things just cannot be done by strength, skill or authority. Even infinite power does not have the ability to create a being which, after its creation, is an *uncreated being*. More power will not help.

In regard to God's creating a stone too big for himself to throw, the first part of the question refers to ability and the second to power. "Can he" and "Is he able" are references to ability, while "too big for himself to lift" and "so heavy that he himself cannot roll it" are references to power. In order to make his point the cynic depends on a collapse of that distinction.

The idea behind onmipotence is not that God has the ability to do everything. He is not able to create a stone too big for himself to move; he does not have the *ability* to reduce his *power*. He cannot do what cannot be done. Infinite power cannot affect anything that cannot be affected by power. God is not able to accomplish those things that require a faulty logic, a certain position or a special relationship that he does not have. The Christian claim is for infinite power, not infinite ability. The claim is that God can do everything that is a normal function of power, not necessarily those things that are functions of other requirements.

From these considerations I think we can derive a definition something like this: *Omnipotence* is the power to do everything that requires power to be done; it is the strength, skill or authority to do anything that requires nothing more than strength, skill or authority to do. Such a definition is not a reversal of classical Christian theology. It is rather a correction of some erroneous ideas about omnipotence that have been generally assumed.

Once we understand that omnipotence refers to power rather than ability, we can easily see some limitations on God's ability that cannot appropriately be considered limitations on his power. It is no reflection on God's omnipotence that there are certain things he cannot do, because there are certain things that power simply cannot do. There are at least three general areas of restrictions on God that I wish to consider, remembering that not one of them diminishes his power nor reflects on his omnipotence.

Logical Limitations

First, there are *logical limitations*. I had an acquaintance whose seventeen-year-old son was killed in an atrocious accident. The following day the mother sat in the funeral parlor, very much outside her normal reasonable self. Standing before the casket, she looked up toward heaven and prayed, "O God, grant that it has not happened."

Could God grant that wish? If the mother had prayed for the son to come alive again, that would have been a different matter. God would then have been asked to do something with the present situation. But he was not being asked to pick up the broken pieces of circumstance and go from there; he was being asked to grant that the circumstance had never existed in the first place. And he was being asked at a point in time after it had in fact happened, by a person who was in that very circumstantial predicament while she was asking.

It might be objected that since God stands outside temporal succession, existing on a level of eternity, he is consequently not subject to the restrictions imposed by time. Nevertheless he was being asked to do *within* temporal succession what is a contradiction. It is a logical absurdity to expect God to "unhappen" what has happened.

Forgiving past sin is something qualitatively different from granting that the sin was never committed. Once the act is done, it will forever have been done. When an evil act is committed, innocence is forever lost. God can make me appear in his eyes as if I had never committed the evil, but I will forever be a person who has committed that evil. Divine grace can extend pardon, favor and restoration of relationship, but even omnipotence can never restore innocence. That would be a logical impossibility.

God cannot create a tiny giant or a gigantic midget, an adult infant or a full-grown duckling. He cannot draw a square circle or build a cubic sphere. He cannot make a totally black body that is totally white, or a surface that is both perfectly smooth and exceedingly rough. Whatever the thing would be cannot even be conceptualized because it is a logical contradiction. What we are saying that God cannot do is not even a "something"; it could never possibly be a something. It is only a nothing that God can never do. He is not limited by logic; he is limited only by illogic.

But someone says, "Since God made the laws of logic, why should he be so restricted by his own laws? Does the lawgiver not stand above his own laws, the creator above his creation? In creating logical laws to which he himself is subject, God obviously divested himself of an element of his power, thus depriving himself of his omnipotence."

That objection, however, is based on a serious misunderstanding of "the laws of logic" and what logic really is. God did not create logic—he *is* logic. To say that he created his own logic is to say that he created his own mind or his own intelligence. He *is* mind; he *is* intelligence. Logic is not the predicate of intelligence; it is the subject of intelligence. Logic *is* intelligence.

It is not that God does not have the *power* to draw a square circle. Power has nothing to do with it. No amount of additional power will help any person come any nearer being able to draw a square circle. The phrase "square circle" contains an internal contradiction and is therefore intrinsically impossible. If you prefer, we can say that a square circle does not have the "ability" to be drawn. The two words are mutually exclusive by definition of the terms, so the phrase is *self*-contradictory.

Moral Restrictions

Second, beside logical limitations on God, there are also *moral restrictions*. *Omnipotence* is a power term; *oughtness* and *rightness* are morality terms. There is a difference between the power to do something and the right to do it. God has the power to do many things that he is not ethically able to do.

Suppose I should try to enlist your help in "pulling off a

job" on the First National Bank. You shy away, thinking I am putting you on until I convince you I am serious. You answer, "I can't." Suppose I consistently rebut all your excuses, but you keep saying "I can't." I say, "Look, all you have to do is hold the bag. Deacon Jones has agreed to drive the getaway car. Your job is simply to hold the bag. Even a child can hold the bag. And you dare look me straight in the eye and tell me you can't? I know you can! What kind of biceps do you carry under your sleeve?"

Suppose I logically back you into a corner until you have only one reason for not helping me. You say, "I can't—because it would not be right." When you have said that, you have appealed to an ultimate principle inherent in the heart of God, and you cannot go beyond it. The greatest reason for doing right is the fact that right is right.

When you said, "I can't," you were not referring to power at all. You were thinking of an ethical principle that constrained you from doing what was not right. Here again we see the difference between power and ability. You had the power but you nevertheless could not do so—ethically you were not able.

In a later chapter we will consider more closely the goodness of God. But assume for the moment that God does have an ethical nature of goodness and rightness. It would be appropriate to say God cannot do what is incongruous with himself. He is morally prohibited from doing what is not right because that would be disconsonant with his own principle of rightness. The limitation on his ability this time is not logical but moral. He "can"—from power, but he "cannot"—because of ethics. His omnipotence is not compromised by the restriction.

Other Restrictions

Third, along with logical and moral limitations there are some self-imposed restrictions on God. They come into clearest focus where freedom is granted to created creatures. It is not that God has voluntarily relinquished the power he once had over his creation in such a way that he cannot regain it. That *would* reflect on his omnipotence. Rather, the Christian view is that God remains in a position to withdraw that freedom at any time. His voluntary surrender had no element of finality; it is not irrevocable and it will not continue forever in the present system. The freedom granted is a continuing thing—for the present only—because of God's continuing choice to surrender certain areas of his freedom to human beings. This notion of freedom will be articulated more thoroughly later on.

These three limitations on God's ability are background for the chapters that follow. We are already beginning to understand why the problem of evil may be less of a problem than originally expected.

4
THE
DIVINE
DILEMMA

IF I SHOULD POLL MILLIONS of persons with the question, "What do you consider to be the highest good in life?" freedom would rank high in priority. In America we have acquired an emotional posture akin to being "drunk with freedom," while politically oppressed societies have been intoxicated with an obsession for freedom. It is easy to cite instances where freedom has been abused with damaging consequences, but for most of us that does not negate the intrinsic goodness we ascribe to the notion. Even with its dangerous liabilities, we would prefer freedom a million times more than the alternative.

God stood in a dilemma, so to speak, when he chose to allow human beings the privilege of moral freedom. Let me personify divine goodness and omnipotence in a scenario that will accent the elements of the predicament. God's goodness "requested" for humanity the good of that freedom, but also requested that no damaging liabilities from the freedom be allowed. In this predicament, divine goodness "appealed" to omnipotence for help. Omnipotence was also in a dilemma. It was able to grant freedom or withhold freedom; it could grant the freedom and allow its abuse or withhold the freedom to prevent its abuse. But the only way it could prevent the abuse was to withhold the freedom. Even omnipotence could not grant real freedom and at the same time prevent its abuse. The request of goodness was beyond the ability of omnipotence to grant.

The dilemma is caused by a logical problem; the inability of omnipotence reflects a logical limitation. If two consequences (good and bad) follow logically from a given proposition (freedom), we cannot expect to have either without the possibility of the other. The two propositions, "human beings are free" and "human beings cannot abuse their freedom," are mutually exclusive, because the freedom to abuse freedom is entailed in the notion of freedom. Preventing its abuse is tantamount to withholding the freedom. Freedom cannot be granted and withheld at the same time. There is no such thing as freedom without the freedom to abuse freedom—without it, freedom is not freedom. If being free does not mean to be that free, then being free has no meaning.

It has been argued that God should have created human beings with freedom to do good but without freedom to do bad. "My boy would have turned out good if a thoughtless God had not given him another option." We cannot say, however, that God "should have" until we have established that God "could have." And we have established just the opposite—that God cannot do what cannot be done. Freedom to do good without freedom not to do good is no freedom at all; that is, it is not moral freedom. It is an absurdity. Freedom by definition entails genuine alternatives and viable options. Freedom to choose good without freedom to choose bad is an illusion. Giving a person freedom to choose while preventing that person from choosing is like making a surface that is both perfectly smooth and perfectly rough. It is a logical impossibility, which does not at all compromise omnipotence. Freedom and constraint at the same point for the same person at the same time cannot even be imagined as a reality—it is pure fiction. Such a nonentity is not "capable" of being actualized; it cannot be affected by power; it has no "ability" to be granted.

J. L. Mackie inquires, "Why should [God] not leave men free to will rightly, but intervene when he sees them beginning to will wrongly?"[3] The answer is that freedom requires options, and the freedom to will rightly without the freedom to will wrongly would not be freedom at all, much less moral freedom. Mackie continues, "If God could do this, but does not, and if he is wholly good, the only explanation could be that even a wrong free act of will is not really evil..." Here Mackie not only assumes that God can do something he cannot do, but makes a further mistake. He confuses a wrong free act with the freedom to do a wrong act. The free act can obviously be wrong while the freedom to make that act can be good. We are talking about two entirely separate things when we speak of an *act* and the *freedom* to act. The one can be either good or bad but the other is by nature good.

The Difference between *Could* and *Would*

Up to this point I assume most of us can agree. We understand why God cannot make persons free to do right who at the same time *could* do no wrong. A more serious objection goes something like this: Why did God not make persons free to do right who at the same time *would* do no wrong—persons who would voluntarily choose right? The assumption is that a person's free choice is determined by the nature or the character of that person. Otherwise a choice would seem to be sheer randomness. Since God allegedly created human nature, he should have built within it a propensity toward goodness with no inclination toward badness.

Of course, a case can be made theologically that human nature *was* created with a propensity toward good. A similar case might be made psychologically, considering the good we see in the world today. Assuming that such a case will hold, it is nevertheless evident that persons do make morally devious choices. Human beings were not created so that they always *would* freely choose what is right.[4]

The freedom here being requested is a freedom to choose in a way that is determined by the "good" character that God supposedly should have created for the person. If God had given me a nature sufficiently good, I would automatically choose good over evil while retaining my freedom. Since God did not make me by nature so pure, I can abuse my neighbor and attribute it to my character—which I in turn blame on God who created it. Thus I am neither accountable for my actions nor culpable for any damage I have done.

The problem with that kind of freedom is that my "free" choice is decided by a predetermined nature, which leaves me with no real freedom. The argument has dead-ended in a logical contradiction. The freedom assigned is "in name only." To say that God could create a nature that would by nature refrain from doing wrong leaves no agent with freedom not to refrain.

If God should create a person who by nature *necessarily* does good, the doing is determined and freedom is eliminated. Such a person would be a robot. To say that the person would do good anyhow, but not necessarily so, means that God would have to stack the deck by overloading the nature so heavily that freedom would be a courtesy title.

To have freedom means that I can make a choice that is uncaused by any factor other than my ability to choose. When I say "I decided to eat the pie," I am thinking of my autonomous selfhood as the ultimate source of my decision. Certainly, other factors may be contributing causes to my choice, including character inclinations, eating habits, hunger, the appearance and smell of the pie and other circumstantial factors. These are contributing causes and often may be sufficient causes. But when I say "I made the choice," I am saying that on this occasion those contributing causes were not sufficient. I see myself as an agent with a predicate that can be called creative autonomy. I myself had the freedom to eat the pie or not to eat it. And all influences on my choice taken together did not add up to a sufficient condition for my action. The influences were determinants but they were not totally determinative. There was a *me* beyond my character condition, with a freedom to choose beyond my own inclinations. Without such freedom a link would be missing in the causal connections that led to my eating the pie.

If a person makes a decision without that decision being determined, that choice is either pure chance or the person has an element of creative autonomy. When a person makes a decision, he or she cannot conceive of the choice being mere chance. The agent—being free from causation and free to initiate causation—furnishes "outside" input into an otherwise mechanistically determined system. That outside input is an uncaused cause.

Now back to the question, "Why did God not create human beings so that they would freely choose good?" The phrase *would freely choose good* is logically contradictory because there is no way a person could be made so that he or she would always choose good without that choice being determined. When *freely* is added to the phrase it becomes contradictory. *Would choose good* assumes that one's choices are determined exclusively by one's nature.

When the choice is thus determined, the freedom has been eliminated from the formula. One cannot freely choose when what one chooses is determined.

The Possibility of Evil

If human beings do indeed have moral freedom, the possibility of moral evil necessarily arises. But that is not to say that moral evil itself is a logical corollary of moral freedom. Moral freedom logically necessitates only the possibility of evil, not its actuality. If that possibility is logically required, however, its actuality cannot be logically prohibited.

The nontheist often argues from *logic* that if God were omnipotent and good, evil could not exist. But in order to argue that way from logic, one must totally discount logic in the original proposition of God's omnipotence. One must say that power is not subject to logic at all, and therefore make omnipotence something terribly illogical. The possibility of moral evil is logically required by moral freedom. To say that God's omnipotence should be able to neutralize that logical necessity is to arrive at one's "logical" conclusion by making God's omnipotence illogical. The argument becomes self-contradictory.

So God was in a dilemma. Even his unlimited, infinite power could not grant what his goodness wanted for humanity—freedom without the liability of its abuse. Moral freedom without the possibility of moral evil was an impossibility. Omnipotence could not help. God was limited by logic. His only alternative was to weigh the good of freedom against its evil possibilities. He chose to grant the freedom with the possibility of evil over refusing the freedom in order to prevent the evil.

It is easy for us to second-guess God and wonder whether freedom under the circumstances is in fact good. This world often seems like an insane asylum being run by the patients. When we contemplate all the evil fallout from wicked people who have abused their freedom, we are inclined to believe that God made an inappropriate choice, that freedom should not be considered good after all. But we get that feeling *only* when we are contemplating the moral evil in the world. When we direct our attention to the good that moral freedom has made possible, we tend to feel that God chose wisely.

Without our freedom there might have been no suffering as we know it, but neither could there have been sympathy. There would have been no hatred, but for the same reason there could have been no voluntary love. There would have been no sorrow, but neither could there have been comfort. There would have been no danger, but neither could there have been courage or heroism. There would have been neither unkindness nor forgiveness. Without moral freedom there would have been no vice, but by the same token there could have been no virtue; virtue that is not freely chosen is no more than the "virtue" of fire to burn, water to freeze or light to shine. Mechanical robots programmed for certain behavior and deprived of freedom would have no privilege of fellowship with God. Both the very worst things in life and the very best are made possible by moral freedom. Freedom itself precludes having the good without the possibility of the bad.

If we could objectively line up the good effects of freedom and its intrinsic value alongside the evil kickback from its abuse, most of us at most periods of our lives in most situations would place a higher premium on having freedom than on not having it. The same choice would be made even by a majority of those who at that very time are suffering from its abuse.

I am aware of how easy it is for me to say these things while I am not experiencing any particular evil. But those who object have probably never appropriated the sheer intensity of good that freedom provides. Christians claim that the dangers of freedom are justified by its rewards, that all the liabilities are justified by its inherent goodness.

We have scriptural reasons to believe that humanity's evil choices have brought even more intensity of pain to the heart of God than to the world. His willingness to continue to grant freedom at such cost to himself is one indication that he is good. Only a good God could grant us the specific privilege of causing so much displeasure to himself. Thus the existence of evil, rather than counting against God, actually indicates to us that God is good. Rather than asking why God allows human beings to suffer, it might be more appropriate to ask why God allows human beings to cause him to suffer.

God's great love for us and our betrayal of that love put a calvary in his heart. He himself has absorbed the greatest kickback from human sin. Suffering awesome effects of our evil acts, a good God continues to give us the freedom to pierce his own soul with pain. In establishing such a relationship with us, God has been daring, courageous, even reckless. Thinking of our eternal benefit, God has not "played it safe."

5
WHY ACCIDENTS HAPPEN

THE MOTHER AWOKE from unconsciousness to discover she had been thrown out of the car. For a moment she lay stunned, her senses slowly returning but her mind still dazed. The few seconds that followed then crescendoed with unimaginable horror. She screamed for her small daughter. The only response she got was silence—horrendous, terrifying. The silence of death. The child's cherubic face was mangled, her body lacerated and crushed. Unthinkable tragedy.

The following day the grief-stricken mother kept asking herself that inevitable question, Why did it have to happen? The question, too painful to express, relentlessly hounded her. At the precise moment to do the most damage, an ill-conceived remark from a thoughtless neighbor complicated the problem and made her grief even more unbearable. "Don't question God," she was admonished. "It was God's will; the child's time was up."

In the last chapter we saw how crimes can be perpetrated on the innocent by the guilty, sometimes intentionally but often inadvertently from selfishness, folly and sin. Such moral evil is accounted for by logical necessity from the notion of freedom. I think one is safe in saying that most of the suffering in the world is directly or indirectly the result of moral evil.

In this chapter, however, we are talking about suffering that results primarily from causal laws of the natural system, such as injuries and accidents.

Causes and Purposes

If the mother had asked, "Why did this happen?" the answer would most likely have been quite simple. The brakes failed, or her car could not negotiate the curve, or an oncoming vehicle was on the wrong side of the road. She would have been asking for a causal explanation: "What caused this accident to occur?"

But instead of asking "Why did it happen?" she asked, "Why did it have to happen?" She was asking for something altogether different from a causal explanation; she was asking for a purposive explanation. She wanted to know the purpose of the accident rather than its cause. Her question assumes that the accident was intended, that there was a definite purpose behind the tragedy responsible for its occurrence. The presupposition is that either God or the gods or fate intended a terrible accident to occur that would take her daughter's life. And her neighbor, too, gave an answer based on purpose rather than cause.

To me it is an enigma that most of us see little spiritual meaning behind the daily events of our lives *until* we get in trouble and have our backs against the wall. Then we start looking for some purpose arbitrarily imposed by a demon god on whom we pin the blame.

If you should ask "Why do you have a sore finger?" you would expect an answer something like "I smashed it with a hammer while I was driving a nail." You probably would not expect an answer like "God purposed that I should have a sore finger," or "The gods planned for me a sore finger in order to make me suffer," or "I wanted a sore finger as an excuse for not helping do the dishes." If you should ask "Why did you smash your finger?" you would expect me to reply "Because I was careless," or "Because the nail was crooked," or "Because the hammer was heavy." You would not expect me to answer "Because I wanted to cooperate with fate."

You can say you have had troubles because God was punishing you, or because God wanted to teach you a lesson, or because he otherwise willed it. Those reasons are purposive. Or you can say you had troubles because you caught a germ or were not careful or did not have adequate foresight. Those reasons are causal. Ordinarily, we accept the cause of an event as adequate explanation for its occurrence without requiring a purpose behind it. As a rule we do not even assume that everything has a purpose.

What do we usually think of as an accident? An accident is not an event without a cause; in an interlocking natural system of causes and effects we can hardly say that anything at all is pure chance. Rather, an accident is an occurrence for which no purpose can be assigned. It is an event that was not intended. Hence we can say that an accident is unreasonable, stupid, absurd and nonsensical. If there were a purpose for the event, it would have been intended —and therefore could not have been an accident.

Certainly we feel sympathetic toward a person distraught with grief who wishes to sort out the pieces of the puzzle to discover a purposive pattern. Sometimes the distress is mitigated by salvaging a little meaning from a tragedy and thus feeling it was not totally in vain. In a later chapter we will see how God can use tragedy for his purposes, which helps diminish the feeling of futility. But saying that God can *find* a useful purpose *in* an accident is not the same as saying God *had* a purpose *for* the accident.

The child died a victim of causal laws, a victim of circumstance. We have reason to believe that her death was an accident, nothing more.

Although we understand all this, our understanding never quite satisfies our need for an adequate explanation. It satisfies only within the context of the natural system of causal necessity. But the human race keeps standing on tiptoe, trying to get a peek beyond the natural system. Our curiosity, our desire to go beyond causal necessity into purposive reasons behind the system, is essentially an indication that we belong to a higher order than the natural. Our intelligence, transcending the structure of our habitat, requires answers beyond the causal system we observe.

Freedom Requires Causal Laws

"Why did the accident happen?" can be answered by reference to natural laws of cause and effect—it is answered within the natural order. But "Why did this have to happen?" is a question about the natural order itself and requires an answer beyond causal necessity. It questions the purpose behind the system, inquiring into its moral justification. I said that God did not purpose the accident to happen, but that is not to say he did not intend to create the natural universe with its causes and effects. The larger question, then, is why God created such a system of natural laws by which children can be killed. Why did God set up a system like that in the first place? Can such a creation, even with the suffering it entails, be justified in a way that would make it compatible with the goodness of God?

Here we need to return to two ideas I have already discussed, the notions of freedom and logical necessity.

Sometimes we admit that human beings have been given moral freedom while completely overlooking the obvious fact that we have also been given natural freedom. We have freedom of movement, freedom to manipulate and use material objects, though this natural freedom is obviously limited by circumstances.

Just as the abuse of moral freedom accounts for moral evil, the abuse of natural freedom accounts for a large measure of natural evil. Natural laws as well as moral laws can be broken. They may be inadvertently transgressed, but when they are broken something happens somewhere.

For instance, a natural law says two objects cannot occupy the same space at the same time. When two approaching cars on separate streets arrive at the same intersection at the same time attempting to occupy the same space, something has to give. A natural law says an object that is unrestrained will move toward the earth. When the law of gravitation is transgressed, someone can get hurt.

These are laws of causal necessity—certain causes require certain effects. They belong to our natural system. We say that God created causal necessity whereas logical necessity is self-existent and therefore uncreated. But we need to see how the two are related at the point of freedom. I am suggesting that *causal necessity is logically necessitated by the notion of freedom*, even moral freedom, and without such causal laws there would be no such thing as freedom of any kind. To avoid creating causal laws God either had to avoid giving people freedom or he had to void immutable logical laws. The latter he could not do; the former he would not do.

In order for us to have freedom, the causal laws might not have to be those of our natural system that we know, but would have to be causal laws of some system something like our natural system and functioning in a similar way. They may not be laws that govern melting and freezing, rising and falling, moving and stopping—laws of material substances as we know them. But the laws would have to be something analogous to our natural laws in that they would have to be causal. And the "substance" on which the laws operated would have to have a stability, a dependability, a predictability as our substances have.

In order to have freedom, human beings would have to be in a position to use those dependable causal laws to cause something to occur. A libertarianism that excludes efficient causation turns freedom into chance and hence ceases to be libertarian. Whatever the causal system might be, if persons are to have freedom in the system they have to be free to *cause* something. This means that the mechanistically determined system must be capable of receiving input from outside causes. Without the freedom to cause something within the system, freedom as we have defined it—the power to determine in a way that is undetermined—has no meaning. My freedom to steal my neighbor's apples is meaningless if, when I shake the tree, the apples do not conform to the laws of gravity and fall off. When people are given freedom within any causal system, they must be free to cause something ugly or cruel to occur.

I have said that a natural system of causes and effects is necessary for natural freedom, and that some kind of causal system is necessary for every kind of freedom. I have said that freedom within any causal system invites the abuse of the freedom, by transgression of the system's laws with the consequent result. Thus natural freedom, or some kind of freedom like natural freedom in some kind of causal system, is necessary for moral freedom. Wherever laws can be violated by the abuse of freedom, the issue becomes a moral one. We have hardly any ways to commit moral evil except in some kind of reference to the causal laws that we are able to use.

I am not arguing that this is the best of all possible worlds. But it is difficult for me to see how any genuine freedom of any kind could exist outside a causal system. And it is difficult to see how any moral freedom could exist without a causal system that allows for the abuse of freedom by the misuse of its causal laws. If freedom does not mean freedom *to cause* what one chooses, it is no freedom. It may be that the causal system we know as our world was *as good* as any such causal system could possibly be before it was infected with the abuse of freedom.

In the next chapter we shall observe more closely the particular causal system that we call our world.

6
CAN NATURE BE EXONERATED?

AFTER WORLD WAR 2 MY DAD purchased an army truck that had been used in the war. I recall how he used that truck to help a neighbor haul in his hay. He used it to take firewood to an old man who otherwise would have had a cold home. The truck served as transportation to bring comfort to an elderly widow. In summertime it was used to take young people in the community to church.

But the same truck had seen action in a devastating war. It had been built to transport combat troops for the purpose of killing. It had been designed as a means to one primary end—destruction.

The same causal laws that make possible a commercial passenger aircraft were used to build the B-52 bomber. The kind of combustion that warms me in winter can burn down my home. The water that breeds fish for our dinner can drown our friends. The physical laws that enable me to build a home for my family are the same laws that enable someone else to build a house to commercialize the bodies and exploit the emotions of young women. The law that makes my downhill journey easy does the opposite for the uphill journey of a person going the other direction. There is a law that keeps my body from sailing out of control into space. But the same law spells out my destruction if I leap from a ten-story building.

Are Causal Laws Good?

So, are such natural causal laws good or bad? Are they intended for bad with only a secondary possibility for good, or were they intended primarily for good with the optional possibility of bad?

I think we can say that the laws themselves are morally neutral. They lend themselves to bad as well as good and to good as well as bad. That neutrality is necessary for the moral freedom of those who are using the laws.

Suppose God had created causal laws that would suddenly become noncausal when employed for morally questionable ends. Cars could be built but not army trucks, passenger planes but not bombers. Combustion could burn firewood but not hardwood flooring or wall paneling. Guns could shoot practice targets but not people. Baseball bats could hit baseballs but not heads. In a way we might prefer such a morally automated world, perhaps leaving human beings with no evil, but also depriving them of their moral freedom.

Natural causal laws had to be created either as morally neutral or morally partial. If they were morally partial, a person using them would be morally neutral—or at least incapable of using them in an immoral way. Such persons might have moral principles but their use of the laws would be nonmoral (because limited), and they would therefore be deprived of the privilege of moral freedom. It is no use saying that such a person could still be morally good in principle. We are talking not about moral principle but moral freedom. It is only as causal laws themselves are morally neutral that those who use them are free to exercise moral discretion. It is a logical thing: either a morally neutral person in a morally automated environment (with no possibility of evil) or a morally free person in a morally neutral environment (with the possibility of evil). But the notion of morally free persons in a morally automated environment is a logical impossibility.

The complex combination of causal laws that produce automobile motion can be used either for an ambulance to save a life or for a getaway car in a burglary. Being morally neutral, the laws are usable for either moral or immoral purposes. Since they can be used either way by me, I have the privilege of choosing the way I wish to use them. I have moral freedom. If the laws would lend themselves to running an ambulance but not a getaway car, I would have no moral freedom in my use of them. Freedom means to be able to cause something of one's own choosing, which requires neutral causal laws capable of being used in such a way—morally or immorally. To ask God to intervene any time a neutral law is used in an immoral or abusive way amounts to the same as asking for a morally automated environment. It is asking that freedom be prohibited.

The question that has bothered some of us, however, has to do with the suffering experienced when causal laws are used inappropriately though in a nonmoral way. Natural laws are often violated unintentionally, even in a way that is unknown at the time. Mistakes are made that are not sins. Toes are stubbed; fingers are mashed; ankles are sprained; hip bones are broken. Brakes fail; stop signs are blown down; scaffolds collapse.

My brevity at this point is not intended to suggest an easy solution. But to me it is simply unintelligible to suggest that neutral, predictable, reliable causal laws could even exist—to provide an environment for moral freedom —without being subject to abuse by neglect as well as choice. If those laws could not be unintentionally violated they would not be dependable. And if they were not dependable they would not provide for freedom. If causal laws are to allow moral freedom, they necessarily must allow natural freedom—that is, freedom within the causal system which in our world happens to be natural. But natural freedom is not natural freedom unless the causal laws allowing the freedom are reliable enough to be violated by neglect or mistake. It was from neglect that the brakes failed. From neglect the stop sign was not anchored to withstand the wind and the scaffold was not adequately supported and braced.

Natural law runs itself in a remarkably consistent way with its interlocking system of causes and effects. The biggest problem we have with nature is our own freedom to make causal input into the system. Then we get the effects of what we have intentionally or inadvertently caused. We stand in a strangely unique relationship with our natural environment. We stand in a position outside the system in being able to create a cause—that is to say, we are in a position to make causal input. In order to enjoy the natural effects of our own causal input, however, we have to stand within the system. Being within the system, we have to suffer the consequences of our own inappropriate or destructive causal input, whether the input has been intentional or otherwise. It would probably be safe to say that nature runs by itself better than it does with human causal input. But it graciously allows our outside input in order to accommodate the human desire to affect our situation.

What about Nature?

Having said that natural causal laws are morally neutral, I think it can be shown that nature by and large does contrive toward human good. The good that I refer to here is not moral goodness as virtue but rather utilitarian goodness as happiness, convenience and usefulness. When human freedom misuses natural laws either willfully or neglectfully, they become dangerous. We transgress the laws and we destroy ourselves against them. But when we use them appropriately they bring convenience, comfort and utility to our lives. If we cooperate with natural laws, they take our astronauts to the moon.

The design of the world as a whole contrives toward human good. Where evil exists it does not seem to exist as the object of the design. Ears are made to hear, not to ache. Air is used to breathe and to cool more than to blow away homes. Sunshine is more for health, vegetable life and human warmth than for sunstroke. Leg bones are for standing and walking and supporting weight rather than for breaking. Apples are for nutrition and the pleasure of eating rather than for stomachaches. You may say there is defect in the design, but the defect is not the object of the design. Even poisonous snakes and preying animals are not calculated so much to cause pain as for protection and survival—and the venom and the sharp teeth have a utilitarian good from the standpoint of the snake and lion.

For the most part the design works as was intended in spite of abusive input from human freedom. We are guilty of gluttonous behavior, but apples in general give much more pleasure than pain. We are careless, shortsighted and neglectful, but many more miles are driven without accidents than with them. Reports of plane crashes horrify us, but for every flight that ends in tragedy there are thousands of flights that end at the concourse gate.

A large part of the defect we think we observe in the natural world is accounted for by logical necessity for human freedom. The freedom includes neglect as well as choice. In the next chapter we will consider those evils that seem to have no relation to freedom at all.

7
VIOLENT ERUPTIONS OF NATURE

SEVERAL YEARS AGO I had the opportunity to view the Mount Irazu crater from the air. That crater had sprayed a city with ashes and soot and ruined the health and property of thousands of people. As the plane climbed through the air pollution over San Jose, Costa Rica, I turned over in my mind the question so many people had asked before: Why do we have this kind of a world?

Probably the most difficult form of evil to justify is the evil and violence caused by nature. Here human freedom supposedly provides no choice. Persons are hurt and killed by earthquakes, floods, tornadoes, volcanoes, and lightning bolts. We are largely helpless in such eruptions of natural violence.

I hasten to say again that I can never pretend to provide

all the answers. At times the pattern of nature looks mad. I am as baffled and bothered as everyone else. After writing this chapter, the problem will remain. What I wish to do is to make a contribution toward the solution, however small it may be. But what I say will be stated in full recognition of two overriding factors. First, these natural evils are responsible for only a small fraction of the suffering spectrum of the human race. Second, in light of our limited access to ultimate truth, what we do not know must not invalidate what we do know; the evil that we recognize must not negate the preponderance of good that we cannot miss.

A preliminary observation has to do with freedom. A very large portion of suffering from these natural evils is the result of neglect or shortsightedness on the part of human beings. Homes are erected below dikes that are unsafe. They are built in the shadows of temporarily inactive volcanoes that are expected to erupt again at an unknown time. Real estate continues to be purchased and buildings constructed even though everyone knows the next volcanic eruption will come without warning. Entire cities built on earth faults are known to be vulnerable to tremors. We know the general shoreline areas most likely to be hit by hurricanes, but we continue to build businesses and residences in those very areas. It is a gamble that freedom allows. The possibility of suffering from such evils is thus logically required from the notion of freedom. Risk-taking accounts for a large portion of suffering from natural evils, but of course it does not account for it all.

Since causal laws of nature are morally neutral, there is no particular moral value, good or bad, inherent in natural effects. We have come to feel that storms and floods are bad, and we refer to them as natural evils. But Nile River floods were considered good for soil fertility by early Egyptians. Grass is considered a weed in the garden but it is good on the lawn. We regard electricity as bad when it takes a life, but we are quick to think it good when it brightens the darkness. We consider lightning more evil when it strikes a neighbor than when it strikes a tree. Even if the tree should be killed, why should it not die from a sudden bolt of lightning as appropriately as from a slower process? Is there any particular virtue to lengthening the process of dying? (That might also be asked regarding human death.)

The Sentient Ingredient
The problem is quite obviously not the eruptions of nature themselves. We cannot say that these natural eruptions are intrinsically evil. I think we generally consider them perfectly appropriate *until sentient beings are affected.* It is their harmful effect on such creatures that we consider an intolerable evil.

We must remember, however, that if humans are going to stand within the natural causal system so as to experience (enjoy) causal effects, they are subject to effects from all the causes within the system—not just effects from the causes they themselves have contributed.

Rather than faulting nature or its Creator for what is nothing more than a natural effect from a natural cause, we need to investigate what seems to be a clumsy relationship between our capacity to be sentiently affected and the natural system that produces the effects. There seems to be a certain incompatibility between the two. It is the sentient ingredient that makes the relationship between us and nature appear to be under such a heavy strain.

Earlier I said that the causal laws of nature are relentlessly dependable and constant and that such uniformity is necessary for freedom. But now we discover a similar consistency in the human body in its ability to be affected by natural causes. Certainly the body is not as predictable in its ability to be affected, but there is nevertheless a measure of consistency in its sentient response.

While reading chapter five someone probably posed the question, "So what?" Causal consistency does not mean that the body has to be rigged to hurt. Why could the human body not have been made with a kind of accommodation to causal laws? Why not a body that is more adaptable to the natural environment, a body immune to pain, a body that would act as shock absorber for the causal effects of natural laws? Could our senses not have been made more elastic, less constant, and therefore less sensitive to pain? Our philosophical or theological problem is not with the eruptions of nature so much as it is with the human body that is so vulnerable to pain. Rather than wondering why the world is not more adapted to human needs, it is probably more appropriate to ask why the human body is not more adaptable to its natural environment. We have been built in such a way as to experience pain; rocks and trees and earth have not.

Before attempting to answer why God has not made the body totally immune to pain, we need to be reminded that it *has* been made immune to a degree that is simply astounding. The human brain carries a built-in self-protection kit that refuses to receive nerve messages from areas of the body that have been too severely damaged. It is a tautology that we cannot suffer more than we are capable of suffering. There are limits to our capacity for pain. Our nerves go into neutral. We get numb. Pain is never proportionate to the force of the blow. The human brain acts as a cushion. There is a resiliency, an elasticity, that allows the body to absorb more causal input with less painful effects. There is really not so much consistency of sentient effects as we originally thought.

When we observe pain sympathetically in a friend rather than experiencing it ourselves, we are sometimes apt to overlook the cushion of the human mechanism, to expect an absolute consistency of sentient effects, and to suppose the pain is in fact more severe than it really is. A bruised, mangled and bloodied body in an automobile accident is a sight too horrible to behold. But what does sight on our part have to do with pain on the victim's part? The chances are he or she is lying there feeling very little, if any, pain at the moment. Without the cushion, pain would be worse than it appears. With the cushion, it sometimes looks worse than it feels. At times we could even wish the body were capable of more pain as a warning signal to withdraw from harmful situations.

Something of a parallel to this occurs emotionally when one is in the throes of mental suffering. Mentally, we "go bland." What appears to onlookers as intensified suffering is sometimes not so concentrated for the sufferer. For the outsider it is focused. For the insider the focus of the suffering is diffused and the concentration is diluted. We become emotionally dull. To a certain extent, suffering is its own anesthetic against itself. If not for that anesthetic, the pain would be as severe as it appears to the beholder.

The same is true with one's capacity to enjoy pleasure. Those who have conveniences do not consistently derive from them the pleasure that a person without them might think. Youth who have had everything money can buy react against material possessions and opt for a simpler lifestyle. A gourmet dinner is more exciting for the one to whom it is new. The resiliency of the human personality is due in part to a measure of insensitivity one develops to one's own condition.

When more pain messages do get through to the brain than the psyche is capable of bearing, the mind usually lapses into unconsciousness. Many more persons could escape from burning homes if they did not become unconscious so soon, an unconsciousness that prevents the experience of pain but also the possibility of escape. The human ability to suffer pain seems to balance on a tightrope between protecting the psyche from too much pain and protecting the body from too little pain. The intensity of pain is a gauge of the body's need for rescue; the limit on the intensity is a gauge of the psyche's ability or inability to withstand. Most of us have a mental constitution tougher than we really know, capable of surviving more pain than we thought possible. For many of us, the psyche has never really been tested.

Even though the human mechanism does carry within itself a certain protective cushion, the question remains about total immunity. To help resolve that problem, I suggest two possibilities.

The Body's Alarm System

First, as already mentioned, the bodies we have been given need pain as an alarm signal to warn of danger. The pain needs to be severe enough to overcome our generally reckless attitude toward physical security. We all understand that. The question is why the bodies we have been given are subject to such danger. We understand why *these* bodies need pain as protection, but why should we have this kind of body in the first place?

To have bodies that would not need pain for survival would require bodies that are unbreakable, unburnable and indestructible. That would mean bodies incapable of being affected by many natural causes. If you reduce the number of natural causes by which one can be affected, you necessarily also diminish the ability to experience pleasure. An unbruisable body could not be affected for good the way our bodies can. An angelic body cannot be hurt by natural causes and therefore has no need for bodily pain, but neither can it experience sensuous pleasures. It is incapable of being affected by physical things. Of course —for all we know—angelic beings may live under some nonnatural system of causes that provides for them something like both pleasure and liability.

Earlier we established that freedom requires some kind of causal system comparable to our natural system. I am now suggesting the possibility that the ability of a body to experience pleasure from natural causes necessitates its vulnerability to injury, and hence the need for pain as warning. Take away the body's ability to respond, and you take away its capacity both for pleasure and for injury. Here we are speaking of causal necessity within our natural system rather than logical necessity. But it may be that within any other conceivable causal system there would be "bugs" as bad as or worse than we think we have discovered in our system.

Love and Freedom

Second, the possibility of pain may be intrinsically required by combining certain qualities. When a son, for instance, conjoins within himself both love from his mother and freedom to reject that love, the possibility of the severest pain imaginable is created for the mother. The sheer intensity of the pain of rejected love is greater for the mother than the physical pain of childbirth when her son was born. When you combine love with rejection, the product is pain. It is a logical requirement from the definitions of love and rejection.

Similarly, combine holiness with freedom to sin and you have the possibility of a pain that offends and stings with inexpressible hurt. Wherever holiness and sin meet, there is always formed a cross of pain—whether in the heart of God or on a hill called Calvary. The product of the combination of the two is sheer pain.

That kind of pain may run through all conscious existence right on into the soul of God, where infinite love and absolute holiness confront rejection and sin in a conflict that produces an intensity of pain unthinkable to mere humans.

Here we are speaking of mental pain, of which the greatest physical pain may be only a shadow. Only those who have experienced the intensity, the severity, of rejected love can know. God has given us the privilege of participating in the soul-stuff of reality, exposing us to the dangerous possibilities of love, holiness and freedom. And I am daring to suggest that God may have honored us by allowing the shadows to concentrate in our lives, a tangible symbol of the reality that otherwise might elude us.

8
WHAT
IS
GOODNESS?

IN OUR HOME WE HAVE imposed restrictions on the general consumption of rich candies. These are rather clearly defined but probably not as rigid as they should be. We are not legalistic about it.

Sometime ago to the surprise of our little daughter I passed around a box of chocolate-coated cherries. And to *my* surprise I received a big exhilarating hug, a bright smile and the welcome announcement: "Oh, Daddy, you're a *good* daddy!"

The interesting thing is that I did not feel any particular virtue from passing out the candy. I probably even felt a slight tinge of guilt. To me, virtue consisted in withholding candy against my desires to indulge my child. I had developed a self-image of a good daddy because I had often withheld temporary happiness for the sake of future and more lasting happiness.

To my daughter, virtue lay in my desire and willingness to indulge her craving for chocolate. I was a good daddy because I gave her immediate temporary happiness, though it may have been at the cost of greater happiness later on. Several times I had attempted to explain my reasons for not allowing undisciplined candy-eating. But each logical conclusion was rebutted with, "But Daddy, I *want* the candy."

Santa or Policeman

Children easily pick up the idea that Santa Claus is good. But somewhere—I hope not from their parents—they often get the notion that police officers are bad. They are inclined to run toward Santa and away from the police. The difference is more than the difference between a bright red costume and a dull blue uniform. I suspect the big difference is that Santa is good *toward us*, but the police expect *us* to be good. There seems to be no virtue in requiring others to be good. Goodness seems to consist in part in willingness to allow us to be bad. It is a popular conception that goodness means giving us the candy we want—whether eating candy is good or bad for us.

Even with this very lowest view of goodness, we might be able to say with certain modifications that God is good. He is good in that he allows us freedom to choose for ourselves the kind of happiness we want and the freedom to pursue that happiness in whatever ways we wish. The modification is that he does not give us the candy that would harm us, only the freedom to go after it ourselves. If he should hand out to us all those cheap thrills that would burn our emotions and grind our lives into dust, he would be bad rather than good. I would be bad to serve my small children a steady diet of rich candies that would harm them.

Utilitarian Goodness

A higher view of goodness is illustrated by a father who wishes for his child a genuine and abiding happiness that requires restrictions or prohibitions on some things that would provide superficial happiness. If the temporary happiness and the greater happiness are mutually exclusive (as they often are), one has to be sacrificed for the sake of the other. The one that is chosen is always enjoyed at the cost of the other.

Goodness is often defined as kindness or beneficence at the point of the lesser happiness with no regard for the greater. Thus we want God to do for us what we are too shortsighted to see we really do not need. And when his higher goodness refuses to do so, we get a chip on our shoulder and complain that God is not good. The soft indulgence of the sentimental "kindness" we think we want would really be easier on God's part to express than what seems to us to be the harsh severity of genuine kindness. God is kinder to us than we may often wish. It is the strength of his kindness that withholds the superficial happiness.

Consequently there may be conflict between the comfort which God may *wish* for his people in the short run and the higher good which he is obligated to *choose* for his people over the long term. Or it may be more accurate to say that he *would* wish their temporary convenience if the higher good were not open. It is the goodness inherent in his kindness which requires human freedom—even with its abuse —because freedom means greater utility than a comfortable, facile existence with no freedom at all.

The difference between indulgent kindness and authentic kindness is the difference between sentiment and love. Real love is a disposition that cuts through sentiment and even through sympathy for the sake of the best and highest good of the beloved. It is that kind of love that prompts a father to withhold from his child a temporary happiness that would derail the long-range designs for permanent happiness. It is that kind of love that we may be tempted to loathe in God, even wishing that he would love us less. But his love withstands the pressures of sentiment, sympathy and the desire to please—for the sake of our highest good.

Goodness and Wrath

In this light we can understand more easily the difficult scriptural concept of the wrath of God. If by wrath one means sudden fits of anger by a person possessed of selfish love with no emotional discipline, then it is not compatible with a God who is good. Because much of the anger we feel as human beings is a corollary of our self-centered desires and selfish love, we are prone to attribute to God the same kind of rage. But in our higher moments most of us experience indignation precisely because we love someone else in an unselfish way. We are hurt if that person settles for less than highest happiness. We are offended if that loved one is abused.

We have generally taken it for granted that wrath is the antithesis of love, so that the more we love the less we are prone to anger. We may think of anger as a corollary of hate. Yet I notice that I become angered by things that happen to my children which do not affect me in the least when they happen to my neighbor's children. I know that an element of selfish love and pride in my children makes part of my anger unjustified. But I have experienced anger that is a pure result of the unselfish love I have for them. I can even be angry with the children themselves for doing things I would be indifferent about in my nieces and nephews, simply because I love my children more.

Every father knows he can be angered at his son without hating him. Anger has very little to do with hate. When one bully is angry with another bully, he is usually angry not because he hates the other bully but because he loves himself and his self-love has been offended. The hate is incidental to the anger; the love is the required ingredient.

When his father discovered that he was experimenting with hard drugs, David was disappointed that he seemed unconcerned. He felt unloved and wished in vain for the slightest trace of anger on his dad's part as an indication of his love and concern. The emotional antithesis of love is not wrath. Wrath is a corollary of love. The antithesis of love is indifference.

If God loved humanity selfishly, he might exhibit the kind of unjustified wrath we consider incompatible with goodness. But if he loves us unselfishly, sacrificially, even at great cost to himself, a kind of holy wrath should be inevitable. That kind of wrath would show his genuine love, assuring us that he is good.

Moral Goodness

Up to this point we have been discussing what is good, and we have placed in the category of goodness those attitudes and actions that make for the happiness and well-being of other persons. It is almost strange, however, to be talking so comfortably about what is good. Our talk about "moral values" betrays an assumption that some attitudes and actions have a dimension beyond what we think of as simply correct, or appropriate, or the best of alternate choices. There is a difference between a person's good *constitution* and good *character*; that difference is a moral difference.

Employer and employee may argue about what is right, but the fact of the argument shows that both agree there *is* such a thing as moral rightness in the case. Each tries to prove his or her point as being in compliance with the principle. That is what the argument is all about. To make the point each person appeals to the notion of the principle recognized and accepted by both.

When we say that a person is morally good, we may be

talking about a personality attribute or a deed, but we are appealing to a principle of moral rightness or goodness that enables us to determine that he or she is good.

What is good can be easily discussed because all agree *that* the principle exists, but the principle itself is more difficult to talk about. The *what* can be defined more easily than the *that*. Ordinarily we simply throw in the term *moral* when we appeal to this higher principle because most people understand what we mean.

The notion of morality can be discussed with regard to character, conscience and motives. When we talk about conscience, however, we are talking about a sense of good and evil emerging in human consciousness. Behaviorists say that the inner sense of good and evil comes from social conditioning. It is my contention, however, that this sense of good and evil cannot be adequately explained without reference to a higher or independent principle of goodness or "oughtness."[5] Let me explain.

From my rocking chair in our family room, I look down through a nine-foot-wide glass wall to sloping woodlands that spread out in all directions. The tree line is actually only a few feet from the house. I see southern pines, late summer gum trees, oaks and hickory. The fact that I visually sense the trees indicates to me that the trees in fact are out there. My sensing of them can best be explained with reference to their actual existence. I am less concerned with the explanation of my senses, however, than with whether the trees are actually there. So I walk out among them, feel them, smell them and hear their leaves dancing in the breeze. My original visual sense was accurate. The trees are there.

When I feel a tinge of guilt, or the satisfaction of having done right, I am doing more than feeling guilt or satisfaction. I am actually sensing that my deeds have either complied with a moral principle or they have not. I sense a principle of rightness perhaps not so clearly but just as surely as I sense a tree. That higher notion of rightness is embedded in human consciousness in the form of oughtness that we call conscience. My sense of good and evil can be explained only with reference to the category of rightness; therefore it points to the category—which I am calling the higher principle.

The analogy of the trees ought not to be pushed too far. No analogy proves anything; this one only illustrates how our sense of good and evil points to the existence of goodness as a principle.

If we say Jones is a good man, we are saying something different from saying an apple is a good fruit or Jones is a good swimmer. The difference is the moral ingredient. If the goodness of an apple or a swimmer is nonmoral, what makes good a *moral* value when used in reference to character? Simply this: the higher principle of rightness. Apart from that principle, the term *moral* has no meaning.

What Is Good?

In the first part of this chapter we discussed utilitarian goodness, goodness which results in long-term happiness. This happiness has a moral value when applied to character or conscience. But long-term happiness is not the only earmark of moral goodness. Other kinds of actions and attitudes are morally good though they may have very little effect on human happiness.

There are occasions, for instance, when truthfulness brings no human happiness and when dishonesty is not humanly abusive. Yet truthfulness is morally right and dishonesty is morally wrong. No reference to human happiness is necessary for something to be moral. Honesty stands for its own sake; it is its own excuse for existing and deserves to be called morally good.

A responsible person is considered morally good in the area of dependability. Being dependable may bring happiness to many persons, but dependability is a morally good quality quite apart from any happiness it brings.

Similarly, we ascribe moral goodness to such attributes as justice, not simply because justice has potential for creating happiness, but because justice is a morally worthy quality standing on its own merit.

The notion of holiness seems to include all these I have mentioned and others. A person who approaches having such moral character begins to develop a propensity toward good things, a liking for them simply because they are good. In contrast, a debauched character may enjoy forbidden fruit and illicit sex not so much for the fruit or sex as for enjoyment of what is forbidden and illicit.

Persons whose characters are moving toward holiness begin to hate selfishness and greed not only because those traits are socially destructive and humanly abusive but also because they are morally wrong. They abhor dishonesty, irresponsibility, injustice and indecency whether those qualities are observed in their children or in total strangers. They are hurt when they see evil—whether or not that evil is damaging anyone they happen to love. Though the distinction may be fuzzy in their own minds, morally inclined persons develop an affinity to goodness simply because it is good, quite apart from their affinity to what may be utilitarian or truthful or dependable. They are able to honor the principle itself. That is the kind of moral goodness we ascribe to God.

I have mentioned several things that can be called morally good because they are matters of character complying with moral principle. Among them are honesty, dependability, justice and utility for happiness.

Conceivably on occasion some "conflict of interest" could arise between the various things we call good, especially in their application to practical situations.

For instance, conflict may arise between justice that requires retribution and mercy that facilitates happiness. We can imagine a situation in which many guilty persons could be spared the pain of punishment by making one innocent person the victim of their crimes. If love is indulgent, the happiness of the larger number of people would prevail at the cost of injustice to the one who is innocent. Similarly, many guilty persons might be exposed by honesty in a way that would greatly reduce their happiness; their happiness could be preserved by dishonesty.

Some of the things we call good may carry more weight in certain situations; if they have more gravity, we say they are higher on the scale of moral value. Whenever there is conflict between values like justice, love and honesty, we are morally constrained to choose the higher moral good in the situation. The highest good cannot be determined simply on the basis of human happiness. On certain occasions, preserving justice and honesty may entail sacrificing the happiness of many individuals.

When we complain that God is not good, I have a hunch we may really be upset because he is *too* good—too good for us. Our soft, sometimes sentimental definition of goodness conflicts with other ingredients of moral holiness. We think we want a God whose goodness is exclusively utilitarian, one who can compromise weightier matters of morality for our happiness. We want to see in him a goodness that is purely human-centered rather than principle-centered. To say that God could not be good and allow human suffering is to define goodness only in terms of human happiness. God is too good for that.

The Source of Rightness

Almost as an appendix to this chapter, we need to inquire about the source of the higher principle of rightness—the category of goodness—that provides us with the notion of moral value. Is it derivative from God's moral nature, or is it an objective principle standing on its own by which the moral nature of God can be determined?

If we say that it is derivative, we have a problem in

claiming that God is good, because we have really not said anything. First, we would have to define goodness as "moral Godlikeness." That would make God himself the standard for goodness, so the proposition "God is good" would be redundant. It would simply say "God is like himself." Rather than ascribing to God the principle of goodness we would be ascribing to goodness the attribute of Godlikeness. God would not intend goodness because it is good, but rather it would be "good" because God intended it. Then the statement "God could not be good and allow evil" would be a contradiction, for if God himself is the standard for moral value he could be "good" and do *anything*. His doing it would make it "good." Conceivably, goodness could then be precisely the opposite of what we know as goodness.

The semantics of what word should be used to designate something altogether different from what we commonly call goodness is not the issue. We are concerned with substance more than semantics. We want to know whether God possesses what we know as goodness, whatever he may wish us to call it.

If goodness is not derivative, the other option is that it is an objective principle standing on its own, by which we can judge the nature of God. This option, which I am strongly urging, is illustrated by our view of logic.

Earlier I said that God is not the Creator of logic, but that he himself is logical. Logic is a principle of intelligence which we find in any rational mind. In a similar way, I think we can say that God is not the Creator of rightness and moral goodness, but that he himself is morally good. Rightness is an ethical principle that we find in the divine nature. It is no more optional with God than is logic. It is an objective principle of morality, just as logic is an objective principle of rationality. God by definition is both logical and moral, meaning that he is rational and ethical. Wherever we find rationality, we find logic; wherever we find morality, we find rightness.

Since God is ultimate intelligence, he is ultimate logic; since he is absolute morality, he is absolute rightness. The principles of logic and rightness are contained absolutely in God's mind and nature as in no other being. When we look for either in its most exemplary form, we look to God. Although self-existent and therefore not derived from God, both are contained in God in perfection. In the same way that we say God is logical, it is appropriate to say God is good.

9
WHAT
IS
EVIL?

WHAT USED TO BE PRETTY WELL understood in our society as moral crime has more recently been reinterpreted without reference to moral principle. Thus *sin* has been redefined as "unsocial behavior," "emotional maladjustment," "inability to cope with one's environment" or even "the healthy eruption of oppressive inhibitions."

Sin is a good word to include in the punch line of a joke. *Wicked* on a theater marquee pays well at the box office. But these words have lost so much of their force that what they stand for is no longer taken seriously. The term *evil*, however, is still a heavy word used with great seriousness.

I get the feeling that sin and wickedness have lost their gravity in our society because they remind us of certain personal actions for which we as individuals are morally accountable. Because we dislike the pressure of moral accountability, we dilute the meanings of the terms.

Defining Evil

The word *evil* is used rather loosely to cover conditions that we consider bad as well as acts and intentions that we consider morally suspect. For lack of better terms I am referring to all such bad conditions—oppressive systems, unbearable situations, even bad apples and rotten eggs—as utilitarian evil. The actions, attitudes and intentions that relate to character and become matters of conscience I am calling moral evil. Thus pain is a utilitarian evil but for me selfishly to cause pain is a moral evil. Suffering is a utilitarian evil but cruelty that causes suffering is moral evil. One is pain; the other is vice. It is true that we think of oppressive regimes as morally evil, but the moral element of a regime is related only to those persons who are morally responsible. The regime is a utilitarian evil while the human oppression is a moral evil.

That distinction is important as it relates to God. Accusations of evil made against God on the grounds of utilitarian evil are often intended to indict him morally. No one seems to care whether God is clumsy, awkward, stupid, crude, inferior or unpolished. He can be a bungling bloke who is all thumbs, a party bore, corny, silly and dull, and no one seems to mind. The charge is not that God is a dud, a clod or a hick. He is accused of moral evil.

In order to move from the utilitarian evil we see in the world to a morally evil God, we would have to establish a causal relation between God and the conditions we observe—thus implicating his character on the ground of his intentions.

Before trying to do that, however, we must come to consensus about what should in fact be considered utilitarian evil in the world. Should the phrase be a canopy under which every undesirable condition is placed? Is it a cover phrase for every nuisance that is even vaguely inconvenient? Is it a condition of ungratified desire even when gratification would produce greater evil? Should the inconvenience of restrictions and prohibitions be considered utilitarian evils even when they are justified? In such a low view, utilitarian evil is caused by a daddy withholding candy so his child will be healthy. Is evil caused by a God who out of genuine concern for our permanent good refuses to grant those temporary conveniences and gratifications that we selfishly want? That view of evil does not warrant a sympathetic treatment in this discussion. Certainly God's ethical nature cannot be called in question on the grounds of the weakest possible view of evil.

A better view of utilitarian evil is possible. It rides heavily on the meaning we attach to a genuinely utilitarian good, because evil is ordinarily considered the antithesis of that: pain rather than pleasure, sorrow rather than joy, misery rather than happiness, illness rather than health, loss rather than gain, ugliness rather than beauty.

Utilitarian evil should also include any damaging condition or situation that cannot be justified in terms of a higher good. It includes mechanical problems, disease and accidents that can be explained only by mechanical or natural causes in our system of causes and effects. Utilitarian evil includes both the pain resulting from cruelty or neglect and the happiness that results from indulgent kindness and cheap sentiment—an unworthy happiness preempting a more permanent happiness.

Of course, it has often been asked whether pain should be considered evil at all and whether pleasure should be considered good. A case might be made that pain qualifies as utilitarian evil only when it is caused by moral evil. Then utilitarian evil would logically follow from moral evil rather than moral evil following from utilitarian evil. In this discussion we are assuming that unjustified pain is indeed a utilitarian evil; hence any attempt to inflict pain is a moral evil because it is an attempt to inflict utilitarian evil.

Utilitarian evil is attributable either to natural causes or to the cruelty or thoughtlessness of persons. Much of it therefore results from either natural freedom or moral freedom. The possibility of such evil is therefore required by logical necessity from the notion of freedom. Those persons responsible are inexcusable, but God can be indicted only on the grounds that freedom is an unnecessary evil. We do not have such grounds for a case against God.

Is Pain Intrinsically Evil?

Now that I have defined pain in general as a utilitarian evil, I wish to back up a step to clarify my conviction that pain is not *intrinsically* a utilitarian evil. If I am correct in that contention, it would be inconsistent to say that allowing pain is intrinsically a moral evil.

To say that suffering is intrinsically evil is to say that all levels of suffering in all possible situations for all possible reasons are evil. It is to say that suffering has no utilitarian value for correction, education or retribution, no value as an occasion for sympathy, comfort and courage. Few people are prepared to say that suffering has no utility for good. Unless we say that, suffering cannot be considered intrinsically evil.

This is not an attempt to explain away the severity of pain. Pain is painful. It can become unbearable. It cannot be dressed up to appear beautiful, spiced up to taste sweet. It is ugly and bitter. When it has become "insufferable," it is suffered more. Pain deserves scathing denunciation. In general it can be called utilitarian evil, but it is not intrinsically so.

In our society I sometimes feel we have become so accustomed to ease, comfort and pleasure that we have an obsession about pain. Sentimentality is mistaken for sympathy, while suffering has a bad press.

If we cannot say that pain is intrinsically a utilitarian

evil, suffering cannot prove that an omnipotent God does not have even utilitarian goodness. Until we can say that allowing pain of any kind is intrinsically a moral evil, suffering cannot prove that God is not morally good.

Moral Evil

Up to this point we have considered moral evil only as the intention to cause or allow the utilitarian evil of pain in a way that reflects on one's character. As in the last chapter, however, we must remember that there are other moral values than human happiness. Values such as truthfulness, dependability and justice have moral merit even when they do not facilitate happiness. Moral evil, then, must be regarded as something broader than merely allowing suffering. When any of these values has been violated, the violation is an act of moral evil whether or not any person is damaged or hurt.

It seems odd that sin is taken so lightly, as something nicely naughty, yet the damaging results of sin are deplored as abhorrent evils that are intolerable. From the Christian perspective, moral evil is a heinous crime not only because it so often causes human suffering, but also because it is diametrically opposed to the moral principle of the divine nature. Moral evil flouts the highest universal standards of rightness which emanate from God and consequently becomes a criminal malignancy in the world. It is so utterly distasteful that Scripture speaks of the "exceeding sinfulness of sin"—its horrible offensiveness incapable of description in any terms stronger than itself.

One wonders whether our society, with its rising crime rate, is not verifying something that should have been obvious all along: a utilitarian ethic that has reference only to the happiness of persons is inadequate as a controlling force in society without reference to a higher divine principle to which we are responsible.

To some persons, for God to be more of a moralist than

a sentimentalist would seem cruel. Yet that is what he is. The final word on God is not that he is love, but that he is holy love. He is righteous love. His "rehabilitation program" was initiated to salvage us primarily from vice and only secondarily from suffering. The purpose of the entire operation, which included Calvary, is more for holiness than for happiness.

Here we find an interesting enigma. God is actually more concerned with human happiness than we would expect from a sentimentalist. He places a higher premium on happiness precisely because he is a moralist. God helps us, not only because he wants us to be happy, but because it is the right thing to do.

The Elimination of Evil

It has sometimes been asked, Is evil opposed by good in such a way that it will be eliminated by goodness so far as possible?

If a yes or no answer is required, the answer must surely be yes. But the question has not been posed in the most appropriate way. Rather than admitting that good is opposed to evil, it would be more accurate to say that evil is opposed to good—so much so that it will destroy itself simply because it is against the good. Goodness is the norm. By its standard other principles stand or fall. Evil will self-destruct because it opposes the good. The psalmist said, "Evil shall hunt the violent man to overthrow him" (Ps 140:11 KJV). Johannes Von Muller, a Swiss historian, said, "Good has but one enemy, the evil; but evil has two enemies, the good and itself."[6]

This process of elimination may be different from what we might wish—it may be long-range rather than swift. But eventually evil must disappear from the universe of a God who is good. It will not even be mentioned in the final chapter of world history. This is the whole point of biblical eschatology.

10
OBSERVATIONS ON PAIN

IN PREVIOUS CHAPTERS I HAVE said that the possibility of pain is required by the privilege of freedom, natural as well as moral. I said that natural disasters pose no problem without the existence of sentient beings that can be hurt, and that the real problem lies in the body's ability to experience pain. On that problem I said that sentient feeling is intended for great happiness in the experience of pleasure, and that pain is intended for physical preservation. I said that within our natural, causal system the body's ability to suffer pain is a measure of the body's ability to enjoy pleasure, that to stand within the causal system for pleasure requires being vulnerable to pain. The package is accepted or rejected as a whole. I said that our natural, causal system may have been as good as any could be before it was infected with the abuse of freedom. I said that the human mechanism has a built-in cushion against pain which prevents persons from suffering more than they are capable of suffering. I have insisted that pain should not necessarily be considered evil.

In this chapter I wish to tie together some loose ends by making a few observations on problems that have not been specifically considered.

Mental Pain

Some time ago I lost half a night's sleep, sympathizing with friends who had been struck with tragedy. The pain burned like fire in my mind and tormented my soul. Why it should happen to hit me at that time I do not know. The irony of it was that the tragedy had happened twelve years earlier and the family had long since recovered. I was losing sleep over people who at the very time were probably sleeping well.

When the acuteness of actual pain is stripped of all the mental pain associated with it, it is greatly diminished. As a child I would expend untold mental energy dreading my next visit to the dentist. The process would sometimes drag on for three months. The actual visit was usually rather brief and the pain surprisingly mild. The entire experience was embarrassingly unworthy of the semiphobia I had developed.

Oftentimes, the pain itself is small in comparison with the associated fear, dread, anxiety, chagrin, regret, self-pity, morbidity, illusions and imaginings. Sympathetic souls sometimes have more sorrow over another person's sorrow than does the suffering person. If we could subtract from the actual pain all the emotional stress of both the victim and the sympathizers, prior to the actual pain and long after, the acuteness of most pain would be greatly reduced. Some of the baggage accompanying pain is totally useless. Imagined pain is a ghoul. Sympathy that becomes morbid is futile. Pity is sometimes paralyzing.

Of course some of the accompaniments are important to have. A healthy sympathy that stings us into helpfulness is useful. It lets the victims of pain know they are not suffering alone. In a way sympathy lifts part of the emotional burden and bears it in one's own heart. It is like saying, "Look, all you have to do is bear the physical pain. I'll bear the rest of the load for you. Please be relieved of the emotional baggage." Sympathy is a form of suffering, and it hurts. It takes courage. That kind of suffering comes not so much from a system God has created as from a logical requirement of the definition of love. Even God is not immune.

Composite Human Suffering

Another observation has to do with the hubbub about "all" the pain in the world. Some "pain philosophizers" are provoked not so much over individual suffering as over the cumulative sum of suffering. It is the total picture of suffering in the world that fires their passions. The implication seems to be that the pain of two persons is twice as hard to bear as the pain of one, that the pain of a million persons is more painful than that of a hundred.

What is overlooked is that no one suffers the pain of a million persons; no one suffers more than one individual can suffer. The pain of a million is no more *intense* than the pain of one. There is as much intensity of hurt from one man dying in a coal mine as there is from fifty. In no way can the volume of pain make its intensity more intense, its painfulness more painful or its suffering more insufferable. No one can suffer more than her or his own suffering.

Only by participating vicariously in the pain of others can one's suffering be compounded by the suffering of many. Only absolute Knowledge and absolute Love could suffer absolutely in a vicarious way for the suffering of the whole world. Goethe said, "If I were God, this world of suffering would break my heart." The Christian answer is that is exactly what the world has done to the heart of God. But God's heart has been just as broken for any one of us as it has been for the whole world.

The Injustice of Innocent Suffering

Some people can accept injustice inflicted on the innocent by blaming it on those who are guilty, while pinning only natural disasters on God. Other people hold God responsible for the entire system which makes possible the suffering of the innocent from the folly, neglect or sins of others.

The system that makes possible my suffering from your carelessness or your suffering from my sin includes two ingredients. One is the "great-human-family" arrangement of society. Human life on earth is arranged on the basis of the whole rather than the individual. The entire human race is one big family with a high degree of interaction and interdependency, with interlocking, reciprocal needs and fulfillment of needs. The other ingredient is individual freedom. It is the unique combination of dependency and freedom which makes injustice possible.

In earlier chapters I have spoken of the value of individual freedom that outweighs its dangers. Here I want to look quickly at the value of interdependence. Suppose life had been arranged on the basis of isolation. I could experience no suffering from your thoughtlessness or cruelty, but neither could I enjoy the benefits of your wisdom or your benevolence. I could have no liabilities from your hate; neither could I have the assets of your love. I would be immune to your badness but unaffected by your goodness. Further, we would have no cumulative knowledge in medical or utilitarian science, no access to any other person's field of expertise, no communication, no fellowship, no love. Each one would be born in isolation, would live in seclusion, would die in solitude. Each would be smothered by his or her own little world with no possibility of breaking out. That kind of life would be intolerable.

God could not prevent the possibility of innocent suffering without rearranging the system—by eliminating either freedom or fellowship. Of course, eliminating interdependence and family life automatically eliminates a large portion of freedom: freedom to help others or to use others, freedom to affect and be affected by others. But again it is a logical thing. Family life cannot be given along with individual freedom within the family without the possibility of innocent suffering from the abuse of freedom.

So entire races are enslaved; ethnic minorities are discriminated against; entire populations are oppressed by ruthless political machines; supposedly undesirable citizens are liquidated; hostages are held; neighbors are used abusively for selfish ends. A cumulative evil effect is built up for succeeding generations.

What are God's options? He could eliminate the human family arrangement, but we could not bear that. He could make mechanical robots of us all by withdrawing our freedom and computerizing our actions. We would never agree to that. He could step in ahead of every damaging human move, but that would be a withdrawal of freedom. He could take away the ability to suffer, but that would entail the loss of more than we are willing to surrender. He could settle the score with each guilty person after each offense. That would sidestep the problem since it would not relieve innocent suffering, though the Christian faith does promise that someday all justice will be equalized. God could himself "make it up" to each offended person and make all the suffering worthwhile. This he has promised to do. This he has done. This he is doing every hour of every day for those who will allow him.

Animal Pain
A fourth observation concerns animal pain, particularly as it reflects a system in which a preying animal's survival

is maintained at the cost of life for the one pursued. Human suffering is more like an exception than the rule, a large portion of it being accounted for by freedom. But in the animal world suffering seems to be the rule rather than the exception because it is built into the system of survival. In the next chapter I will consider the traditional Christian view of the Fall of nature. Here I wish to point out that in the animal world inflicted pain is on the whole far less characteristic than we sentimentalists ordinarily think.

To some readers I may sound harsh, almost cruel, minimizing the painfulness of pain, with little sympathy toward any pain that I myself have never suffered. My own confession, however, is that I am a sentimentalist, too much so. I am not a fisherman because it hurts me to place a live worm on a hook. It grinds my heart into hamburger to feel the tug of a bass that is hooked in the throat.

Notwithstanding my softness and sentimentality, I must admit that to see the wild kingdom as a scene of perpetual violence and torture requires lenses that magnify things to exaggerated dimensions. That picture is as untrue to nature as is a Winnie-the-Pooh book depicting different animal species in friendly dialog. What appears to us as overwhelmingly offensive terrorism is primarily in our imagination—it comes from imagining how we would feel if we were in the same position. But we are not animals and animals are not human, and there is no reason to suppose the two would experience the same thing to the same degree in the same situation.

Physical pain requires both nerve sensitivity and a mental consciousness to pick up and read the nerve messages. Intensity of pain depends on the degree of development and refinement of both nerve sensitivity and mental capabilities. Although the efficient cause of pain may be outside, a necessary condition lies within the organism itself. The intensity of pain is limited by the capacity of an organism to experience pain. Within the animal kingdom exists a whole graduated scale of pain-experiencing capabilities. The higher forms of life have much greater capacity for suffering than the lower. The point has been clearly made by authorities in the field, so it does not need detailed reiteration. Animals are "blessed" with the absence of human sensibilities. As we ascend the scale we find increasing capacity for pain. At the bottom is no pain at all. At the top is a Cross. In the animal kingdom we find an interesting pattern: The lower an animal's capacity for suffering, the more of a prey it is. The higher the suffering capacity, the less of a prey.

Duration of life cannot be a point in objecting to animal suffering. Quick termination of life may be the least undesirable kind of death. An animal seized as prey escapes a long, dragged-out deterioration from disease and age. Considering the alternatives within the family of animals, that begins to look like the most merciful kind of death. Although we call it violent, such a death is ordinarily accompanied by very little pain. Quite probably the emotional shock experienced by a seized animal is like an anesthetic allowing the victim to die in a state of anesthesia.

Further, the problem of physical pain among animals is not compounded by mental pain, which is often associated with human suffering. Our kind of sorrow, disappointment, despair and grief is almost unknown among animals. They experience no prolonged terror. Jungle murders are seldom bungled. Pursuit and flight amount to the regular employment of many species, which seem to get a measure of joy from the competitive game. Their emotional feelings seem well adapted to their employment. On the whole the wild kingdom seems to carry a general disposition comparable to what we would call an attitude of happiness.

11
DIFFICULT
SCRIPTURAL
ANSWERS

WHEN ATTEMPTING TO COMMUNICATE with nonbelievers about the problem of evil, Christians are faced at once with an important decision. Either we invite others to discuss the problem on our own territory, or we move to the "turf" on which they have homesteaded. We begin the discussion either from our standpoint or from theirs.

In this regard it is usually easier to be a guest than a host. The guest is the challenger on the offense; the host is attempting to hold ground defensively. Over at your place I am the aggressor, questioning your position; you are standing trial. As soon as we move to my place, I am on trial and my position is vulnerable. So I dig in, block up the trenches and refortify the garrison.

The subject of discussion in this book more or less automatically moves over into my area for defense. It is the nonbeliever who questions the goodness of God in the face of evil; the Christian is expected to provide an answer. Early in the book I attempted to shift ground by describing the problem as a *relatively* inconsequential matter in relation to the larger "problem" of good. But as soon as we returned to the problem of evil itself, apart from its relationship to the problem of good, we were back at my place. The nonbeliever's challenge required of me a defensive role. So far that defense has taken a form calculated to elicit favorable response by beginning with premises one can accept more easily than some of the traditional Christian premises. I have attempted to use models, language and thought patterns with which the nonbeliever feels comfortable—the "logic of man" rather than the "logic of God," as John Wisdom would say. I have attempted to play defense "offensively," challenging the other position and attempting to avoid with agility some of the distinctive Christian answers most vulnerable to outside attack.

Sooner or later the time comes when Christian distinctives must be stated and defended. It is not easy to make them plausible to nonbelievers, primarily because such individuals stand outside the Christian arrangement of truth. The difficult Christian distinctives are much easier to accept from within the system than from outside. They are quite easy to accept when they come with the whole package because then they are seen in perspective. Standing on their own, outside the orderly arrangement, they seem implausible.

So I am making myself vulnerable by inviting the nonbeliever over to my area; I am inviting her or him to consider as sympathetically as possible *from the Christian standpoint* the ideas of a personal devil and nature's Fall. Even if we cannot understand the problem of evil philosophically, we can look at it theologically. By that I mean that certain truths can be arrived at by revelation that make perfectly good philosophical sense, though they cannot be arrived at philosophically. Any readers who may have come a bit nearer to the Christian position but still cannot accept all that is in this chapter are urged not to surrender the areas where we have already agreed.

The World Is Out of Gear

To me the Christian faith sounds fully authentic when it freely admits without reservation that something is drastically wrong with the world—that the cogwheels have slipped, the gears are stripped. No attempt is made in the Judeo-Christian Scriptures to conceal the problem, "stonewall the evidence," minimize its importance or look the other way. Rather, the Scriptures are specifically preoccupied both with exposing the problem and with providing a remedy.

Looking at the world, I am struck with two inescapable forces that I observe, sometimes operating side by side but more often in the tension of conflict. I see the underside of a rug with tattered edges and ragged ends, bumps and knots and a distorted pattern like something I would expect a maniac to make. But as I look closer I see a design, a purposeful pattern. It is distorted, to be sure, but it is unmistakable. Now, with the pattern looking more like the product of a wise and experienced rug maker, the distortion looks like the work of either a novice or an enemy.

When I observe the world, I see something like a painting by an accomplished artist, which has torn edges, punctured canvas and scratched surface resulting from later tampering, neglect or misuse. The world is like an old automobile with bent fenders, cracked windshield and broken glass. Obviously, at one time it was something of grace, beauty and utility before a reckless driver got behind the wheel.

Nature, even as we observe it, has intricate evidences of the wisest, cleverest and most beneficent intelligence, yet it looks like a commodity that has borne the strain of an enemy or some alien ingredient for which it was not made. The natural causal system appears to have had some outside input which nature was unable to accommodate congenially. The outside forces have produced inside effects unsympathetic to the life in the system—the kind of life that had originally been fit to absorb with ease all effects from causes within the system.

A great deal of the tension we observe between life and its natural surroundings is due to the causal input human freedom allows. Prostitution of our natural environment has made wildlife subsistence hazardous and precarious; human cruelty has disrupted and distorted the whole natural pattern. The human abuse of freedom is theologically referred to as the Fall of man—it is the predicament of human beings having used their freedom to rebel against God. The Fall of nature is roughly the natural consequence of the human Fall. Humankind held their natural world as a trust from God, so when their relationship with God was disrupted their relationship with the environment was distorted. The discord between human beings and nature reflects the tension that has developed between them and God. When the foundation cracked the entire frame slumped. When the children rebelled against their father they began to tear the house apart.

A Foreign Intruder
Yet there is obviously more wrong with the world than the causal input from humanity. This world has been debased and vulgarized beyond human ability. If we were less sophisticated we might even think that some sinister force just out of sight was consistently programming the world with evil. Many claim to have a cosmology so "cultured" or "developed" that it will not allow them to believe any such personal, sinister force could possibly exist.

On the other hand, I cannot intelligently claim a cosmology so narrow as to preclude the possibility of other living beings in the universe, existing in dimensions of which I have never dreamed. I cannot cynically dismiss the possibility that such beings may have a kind of moral freedom like ours. And I cannot consistently admit that human beings have abused their freedom without allowing for the possibility of the abuse of freedom by other free beings— who may be greater in all ways than we.

Certainly we know that the whole interlocking cause-and-effect system of our world is capable of absorbing outside causes to produce effects within the system. I illustrate this every time I decide to lift a hand to throw a pebble or lift a foot to kick a ball. If there were a high and powerful creature existing in a dimension beyond empirical verification by my five senses, and if he were "fallen" from the most ethical and moral use of his freedom in such a way that his inclinations were wholly toward evil, we do in fact know that our world is capable of receiving any causal input that he would be in a position to give. From the standpoint of our causal system, there is no limit to the effects that can be received from outside input—moral, immoral or amoral. Our world stands in a situation vulnerable to any and all causes that can possibly reach our territory.

So far we have admitted that we must be broad enough to embrace a cosmology allowing the possibility of such an evil, fallen creature capable of causing evil effects in our world, and we have admitted that our world's causal system is dangerously vulnerable to such an invasion. We have also admitted that the awkward relationship between good and evil in our world looks—at times, anyhow—as if a world intended for good has been infected with an alien, evil influence. At times we are inclined to feel that the evil programming of our world even looks "masterminded." All this, of course, does not prove the existence of a foreign evil intruder. But the possibility of such an occurrence is not at all so incredible as we may have thought.

For Christians the one additional piece of evidence forc-
ing itself on us with irresistible force is the teaching of
Jesus. No juggling of theories about what he meant can
alter his unmasked, straightforward teaching about an evil
personality called Satan. To Jesus it was not a theory. Satan
was real, brutal and clever. Jesus had seen him, confronted
him, battled him on a mountaintop. Jesus' words do not
have the sound of a dreamer or a mystic, but of a person in
a life-and-death struggle for the world's soul. Jesus knew
what reality was all about.

The authentic Christian image of Satan is not a horned
monster with sharp tail, pitchfork and the scowl of a vil-
lain with smoke curling around his grimace. Rather, it is
the picture of a one-time creature of brightness and beauty,
strength and wisdom, whose total personality is utterly
corrupted with hatred, forever railing in bitterness against
rightness, goodness and God. Satan is a "fallen angel,"
representing the ultimate liability entailed in the privilege
of freedom.

Christianity does not delineate in detail all the ways that
the master of evil is capable of effecting evil in the world.
Whether he is in a position to cause natural evil effects
such as storms, earthquakes, accidents or diseases, we do
not know for sure. He is in a position, however, to influence within certain limits the decision making of other
morally free persons and thus indirectly, through morally
fallen followers, to fill the world with evil.

And this alien may be in a position to influence within
limits even animals that have a certain measure of natural
freedom. If so, his influence may account for certain species having become carnivorous that may have originally
been created herbivorous. All of that may be part of what
should be called the Fall of nature.

The Subversion Overcome
Beyond such conjecture, the Christian Scriptures promise

a day when all evil will be eliminated, all injustices cor-
rected, all pain and tears abolished. The subversive coup
will be overthrown. The rebellion will be put down. Nature will be restored to its intended purity, and what we
call natural enmity will disappear.

> The wolf shall dwell with the lamb,
> and the leopard shall lie down with the kid,
> and the calf and the lion and the fatling together,
> and a little child shall lead them.
> The cow and the bear shall feed;
> their young shall lie down together;
> and the lion shall eat straw like the ox.
> The sucking child shall play over the hole of the asp,
> and the weaned child shall put his hand on the adder's
>   den.
> They shall not hurt or destroy in all my holy mountain;
> for the earth shall be full of the knowledge of the LORD
> as the waters cover the sea. (Is 11:6-9)

Until that day Satan is fighting like mad to do all the damage he can, knowing that someday all heaven will break
loose!

12
DIVINE INTERVENTION

I SAT IN THE OFFICE of a wealthy businessman who was telling me as a fellow Christian some of his secrets of financial success. "All I have to do is obey God," he announced, "and the money comes rolling in." I rejoiced with him in his success and joined him in giving God the credit. All the while I was wondering to myself whether I had really been so proportionately disobedient. But I accepted his testimony as a statement both of fact and of faith without any inclination to dispute.

His next statement was something altogether different. "All a person has to do is obey the Lord." There he made a statement of opinion by giving a universal application to his own limited experience. If everybody obeyed the way he obeyed, would they all have the wealth he had? I recalled some dedicated Christians who had suffered material loss precisely because they had been obedient to God. For them, being Christian meant they had to change a company policy, which greatly limited their income, and then had to redistribute some of their wealth.

"God healed me," a friend reported, "and I know he will do it for you." The second clause was a conclusion mistakenly inferred from a premise we have no reason to doubt. Because God does something for one person at one time does not necessarily mean he will do it for the same person all the time or for all persons at any time. The second idea does not follow from the first.

In this chapter we are considering the occurrence of miracles—and also why they do not occur more frequently.

Are Miracles Possible?

We need to begin with the understanding that nature has been set up to run rather well. It is not set up in such a way that every natural event requires the direct hand of deity to move it (as is believed in nature religions). The system by which nature is able to run itself is called the causal system, or the system of causes and effects. Every natural event is caused by a prior event, which in turn was caused by a still prior event. Each event is an effect of a previous cause, but the effect then becomes a cause for a succeeding effect. Thus we have successive events that owe their existence to a cause-and-effect chain. Many events are effects of more than one causal chain that converge at the same time and place, producing the occurrence. The process is complex, but it is nevertheless mechanical and precise, at least on the macro-level where the events we normally experience occur. Therefore such events are theoretically predictable.

The system was set up originally by God and continues to exist because of his creative power. As the One who made the initial move producing the first effect, he was the "uncaused cause." God is ultimately behind the events that occur and is responsible for the system by which they occur. But because the system was given the ability to run itself once it was begun, the specific purpose of God is not immediately and directly behind every natural event.

The system is so arranged that it is able to take outside input from nonnatural (transnatural or supernatural) causes. A nonnatural cause from outside produces a natural effect, thus beginning a causal chain of succeeding interlocking events within the system. The events produce other events and the causal chain converges with other causal chains to produce other events, all within the natural system. The outside input (nonnatural causes) is from beings endowed with creative autonomy which we call freedom. Such beings are free to create a cause and to place it into the system.

In human beings our creative initiative is in our minds, operating on nature every time a hand is "miraculously" moved by nothing more than a simple mental decision. In our world we have some four billion persons performing such "miracles" many times every day, tinkering with the natural system, manipulating events, autonomously programming the world with outside causes. With so much human freedom affecting the world of events, we can easily understand that God is not directly behind every occurrence, nor is he necessarily pleased with all events taking place.

When we are suffering a throbbing headache or toothache, we are sure we would prefer a system in which every event would be totally directed by God. But as soon as we regain our health we switch back to being quite happy with a system that we can manipulate ourselves, thank you.

I am taking the liberty to define *miracle* as the occurrence of any event from a nonnatural cause. Divine miracle is the occurrence of an event from a divine cause. It is not an arbitrary superimposition of a super law in a way that temporarily deactivates natural law, but rather it is divine causal input into the natural cause-and-effect system. The natural law continues to operate by picking up whatever causes enter its domain from whatever source and allowing nature to be appropriately affected. Divine miracle operates within the context of natural law. If a miracle seems to be a suspension of the natural law of cause and effect, it is by introduction of an additional cause strong enough to produce an unexpected effect. The causal necessity we see in the natural system, far from excluding divine miracles, is in fact the means by which miracles can occur.

If God created the world so as to be able to receive contact and influence from outside sources, so as to be affected by persons with freedom and even by an outside evil personality, surely he left the world with an ability to be affected by his own divine causes. The extent of such divine input, the nature of it and its frequency are other questions. But the fact that he made the world affectable should have been expected. The fact that divine miracles have occurred and do occur should not be surprising. Every prayer regarding a natural matter that is answered in a tangible way is a miracle.

Should Miracles Be Expected?

Sometime ago I was hobbling around on crutches with a badly bruised ankle when a friend glibly remarked, "God can heal it for you right now." The fact that I was on crutches indicated to my friend that I did not believe it. It so happens that I had never seriously entertained a doubt that God *could* heal it. To me the important question was, Might God have some reason utterly unknown to me why he would not wish to do it now? Certainly I wanted it healed immediately; I did not want the inconvenience of confinement and immobility. Now, of course, I do not mind at all that it healed slowly by natural processes rather than immediately. Why did it seem so important to eliminate the inconvenience at the time? If it is not important to me now, could it really have been important then?

My two-year-old son was irritated that I did not repair

his toy truck immediately—simply because he had his mind set on playing with it. There was no use trying to explain to him why I could not do it at the moment; he would never understand. Switching his interest to another plaything did not give him half the discomfort that he expected. I fixed the toy eventually and when I finished it was good as new.

We think God has to do everything our way and in our own time, not allowing him to have any ideas about the situation at all. We have taken certain values of our culture—wealth and health—and have blown them up into superspiritual values. The church has lost its intended position as a subculture and a counterculture. When divine miracles serving physical and material values become our greatest "sales pitch," the church's appeal is reduced to that of a Madison Avenue commercial.

As soon as we learn that God is good, we begin scheming to use his goodness for selfish advantage. We want to dictate his policies, give him instructions, use him as an errand boy. We try to blackmail him by accusing him of not being good when he does not obey our directions. We keep asking him to play our game our way, to accommodate our desires. We want to be lord and master over God himself.

Yet if God is God at all, he is supposed to be God *over* us; we are not in a position to be gods over him. It is hard for us to realize that his repairing our toys is his department rather than ours. Answering our prayer is his to do or decline, not ours to maneuver him to do. He is not manipulable and his department is not ours to manage. Repairing our toys in our preferred time or his, even repairing them at all, is a prerogative that belongs totally to God.

Parenthetically, I should add that only those prayers regarding natural, material or physical matters are asking for divine input into the natural causal system. Sometimes God answers such prayers through other persons or even through the ones who pray, if they are in a position to place the required input for the desired effect. Sometimes he does it himself directly. When we pray for grace, forgiveness, patience or moral strength, we are praying for a spiritual effect in our lives which does not require divine input into the natural causal system. Even these prayers, however, may be answered through natural causes that provide the occasion for spiritual effect on our personalities.

The problem with expecting constant divine miracles to remedy all sorts of unpleasant situations is simply that such expectations are disappointed. We do not see such miracles occurring constantly even in some of the noblest Christians. Physical suffering is not regularly checked; troubles are not always intercepted. And the Scriptures do not lead us to any such expectations.

The apostle Peter wrote: "The eyes of the Lord are over the righteous, and his ears are open unto their prayers. . . . And who is he that will harm you, if ye be followers of that which is good?" But in the very next phrase Peter added, "But and if ye suffer for righteousness' sake, happy are ye" (1 Pet 3:12-14 KJV). Again he said, "If any man suffer as a Christian, let him not be ashamed," and "Wherefore let them that suffer . . . commit the keeping of their souls to him" (1 Pet 4:16, 19 KJV).

For the sake of the record, I am convinced that more of us would see many more divine miracles than we do if only we were more diligent in our prayers, stronger in our faith and more carefully obedient to God's purposes in our lives. But to create the constant expectation of easy miracles is to do great disservice to those blind, deaf, invalid and otherwise afflicted persons who are more dedicated to God than many who have the blessing of health or even the miracle of healing. Terminal patients are sometimes conditioned for discouragement, disappointment and even despair by thoughtless promises and false hope. They are made to feel as if the rest of the Christian world considers them second-class Christians because they have not been healed.

The writer of the epistle to the Hebrews listed some of the positive benefits of faith. It was through faith that kingdoms had been subdued, the mouths of lions had been stopped, fire had been quenched, the sword escaped, enemies conquered, battles won, the dead raised. These were miracles. From that delineation we might get the idea that faith is a magic wand to change a pumpkin into a golden coach. But in the very next sentence the writer said that others were tortured, mocked and scourged, imprisoned, stoned, sawn asunder, slain with the sword, afflicted, tormented, lived in dens and caves, all of whom "obtained a good report *through faith*" (Heb 11:33-39 KJV, italics mine).

I have no doubt that many are healed by divine miracles through faith. I am also convinced that many are "healed" by mental suggestion. There is a big difference between New Testament faith and having a mind vulnerable to suggestion. Christian faith requires mental discipline and a quality of mental toughness as well as intellectual humility. Mental suggestibility reflects sloppy thinking and leaves the mind vulnerable to evil suggestions as well as good, falsehood as well as truth, superstition rather than objective conceptual reality.

Why Not?

So why does God not always heal through instantaneous miracles those whose lives are committed to him? Certainly no earthling is in a position to know all the reasons, because we have access only to that portion of God's thinking that he chooses to place within our field of discovery. My brief suggestions on this point are stated as mere speculation—as what I am inclined to believe without any feeling of certainty at all.

The primary reason, I suppose, has to do with God's method of running the world. The advisability of the method may be questioned or defended ethically, though all God's reasons for the method may not be known to us. The method we observe operating in the world reflects the arrangement of nature to run itself with little divine tampering. It looks as if God has wound it up and allowed it to unwind itself through a system of causes and effects.

That sounds like deism, but deism claims that God has taken no interest in the world since the time he set it in motion. I am saying that God remains greatly interested and is operative in ways of which we are not always aware. He is functioning in the world in a spiritual dimension, in the minds, consciences and emotions of persons in a way that requires no direct causal additive to the natural system. Additionally, on occasion, he operates within the natural system by causal input, which we call miracle. Such miracles of protection and preservation may be more common and numerous than we think.

The point is that miracle is not God's general *modus operandi*. The entire natural causal system would be superfluous and even redundant if God managed everything directly. What we observe as the uniformity of nature would be an illusion, and the appearance of dependable, calculable natural laws would be a mockery of the notion of freedom—if God's mode of operation were constant "intervention." Before we expect from God too much interference, we should remember that the natural causal system itself is his own creation. Natural laws governing processes of physical restoration and health are his laws, so God's general method of healing is perfectly appropriate to his own created system. To ask him to intervene is to expect him to intercept his own laws and to suspend his general procedures. That is true not only when the natural causal laws effect a slow, systematic recovery but also when they lead to the cessation of life. To ask for healing is appropriate to our relationship with God as his children, but we must remember the gravity of our request. We are asking him to break his own general rules to perform an exception on our behalf. Many times an exception would have to be made at too great a cost to the system through which the human family finds security and freedom.

A miracle of divine healing has certain incontestably positive values—value in increasing and confirming the faith of the beneficiary, value as a witness to the world of divine activity in human life as well as the utilitarian value of reducing suffering. When we cooperate with God in our suffering, however, the process has the potential of carrying us further in certain areas than health could ever carry us. More faith and courage are often required to withstand suffering than are required for healing.

Rather than asking why God does not *always* heal by miracle, it may be more appropriate to ask why he should *ever* heal by miracle. The answer may be that those who are weak in faith and courage may need such a miracle. Those who languish may need a prop to lean on. Those whose confidence in God is weakening need a boost for their faith. Jesus rebuked the Pharisees for requiring a sign (Mt 12:38-39). To experience a miracle does not necessarily indicate spiritual maturity, great faith or special status with God. It may on occasion reflect special weakness and immaturity. Suffering is often a more accurate indication of courageous character and mature faith than health or healing.

One of the most beautiful Christians I ever knew spent the last several years of her life as a terminal patient before her life finally expired in her midfifties. She was my mother-in-law. As a side effect of her cancer, Mildred Black developed a tickling in her throat that produced a chronic cough. It became very annoying. We had prayed for her recovery from cancer, simply assuming that an answer to the prayer would also eliminate the coughing. She did not recover.

One morning sitting at her breakfast table alone, she prayed a simple prayer. She asked for relief from the vexing cough. There were no "professional" faith pray-ers present, no laying on of hands. Just a simple prayer from a Christian who was committed to God. Immediately she felt something move in her throat as if something had happened. Simultaneous with the movement was a disappearance of the tickling. It was sudden, precise and definite. She lived two more years, and the cough never returned. She was healed of the cough. She was not healed of the cancer.

Sometime during the week before her death I sat alone at her bedside. She was weak and talked with difficulty. I asked whether her mind was active during the long vigil of waiting, a wait that had spread out like empty space. I wondered whether she could throw her mind into neutral.

I was not prepared for her answer. She was spending those long hours praying for the health and healing of her friends who were ill. Resigned to the inevitability of her own death, she now occupied herself with prayers for her friends. She still believed in God, she still believed in prayer, and she still believed in believing. She was not healed, but she believed in healing.

In that room that day I saw a stronger faith than I have ever seen in anyone who has been healed. Out of the ugliness of her own suffering, something emerged that could not possibly have been so beautiful against any other background.

13
PUTTING SUFFERING TO USE

EVIDENTLY GOD USED A communist regime in Indonesia to prepare the way for Christian evangelization. We have no reason to believe that God purposed such a government for the Indonesian people, but once it was there he was able to use it for his purposes.

God used some of the evil kings of ancient Persia and Babylonia to accomplish his own goals when they did not even suspect they were being used. The God-fearless Pharaoh of Egypt was used by God to provide an occasion to demonstrate his power. The psalmist sang, "Surely the wrath of man shall praise thee" (Ps 76:10 KJV).

As a general rule, I think we should not say that God allows suffering simply for the purpose of being able to use it. He allows it, first, because he ordinarily chooses to let the natural causal system operate, so that the system will remain dependable enough to accommodate both personal freedom and public utility. He allows it, second, so that the pain may fulfill the purpose for which the human body was made subject to pain: to be used as an alarm system to warn of danger. Pain must be severe enough to overcome an often careless attitude toward self-preservation.

Beyond these reasons, God does not make a general rule of allowing suffering for the special purpose of facilitating what he has in mind to accomplish in our lives. But once suffering is present, God wastes no opportunities to use that suffering for redemptive purposes. The fact that suffering has many positive values can hardly be denied, though we cannot go so far as to say it is intrinsically good. What is good in suffering is not the suffering itself, but its positive effects. Consequently pain is never divinely allowed purely for pain's sake. Allowed for the reasons stated above, it is used for a broad range of purposes, both moral and utilitarian.

To discover these worthwhile purposes and put our suffering to creative and constructive use is like finding the handle to turn a dagger that would otherwise destroy us. Harmful effects are more than neutralized. Liabilities become assets. From Beethoven's deafness came some of the world's musical masterpieces. From Milton's blindness we have *Paradise Lost* and *Paradise Regained*. Out of the worst in life can come the best. Something ugly is transformed into something beautiful; something destructive into something beneficial. Discords become music. Suffering becomes sacramental.

In this chapter I want to suggest several positive benefits for which suffering can be used, benefits that God may be attempting to effect through our suffering.

Character Construction and Personality Building
First, suffering is used for building moral character. Every obstacle course builds muscle; every steep climb increases

lung capacity. Trials handled successfully deposit new power and strengthen spiritual nerve. When bitter testing and severe trial produce positive decision, one's character grows stronger.

During my high-school days on a farm in Alabama, I took pride in being a plow hand with a workhorse and stockplow. In early spring, blisters would appear on my hands from gripping the plowstaff. Long before "laying-by time," however, the blisters would go away and in their place would appear calluses, tough as hardened leather. I learned that the hardness always comes at the point of contact with the friction. Toughness comes where the rub occurs.

But sometimes we wonder why God would set up the program so that character can best be built through obstacles. Why should his character-building program include pain? The answer, I suppose, would be, Why not? What is specifically wrong about allowing pain, difficulty and opposition to strengthen character? Logically, it may be true that the rewards would be cheap without it. Whatever is without cost is worthless, and whatever is worthwhile is costly. At the point of eternal salvation, God himself paid the price because it was too expensive for us to pay ourselves. Hence it is easy for us to take his Calvary sacrifice for granted. Salvation sometimes seems cheap to us, though for God it was costly in suffering. Other values in life would seem cheap to us without the cost of inconvenience, sacrifice and suffering.

It might be easier for God to give us character than to help us develop it ourselves, but it would not be worth as much to us. It is easier for me to tie the shoes and zip the coat of my small son than to have the patience to let him do it for himself. My willingness to stand back and watch him work through his clumsiness to do something difficult is not an indication of weakness, inability or lack of consideration on my part. Rather, it is a sign of maturity, strength and love for my boy. He wants me to stand back and wait. And he enjoys his zipped-up coat more when he has done it himself, precisely because it was hard for him to do.

I have not said that God allows suffering primarily for character building. I have said that he does use suffering for that important purpose. Pain, trials and difficulties in life provide the occasion for us to develop the character to stand tall, live right, walk straight and be true. And the character thus developed rates a higher premium in our own values.

Second, most of us not only need stronger character, but we could also use a more congenial, more sympathetic, more Christlike personality. The early Israelites found honey in the rock. Our convictions need the texture of granite but our sympathies need the sweetness, softness and lubricating quality of honey. Rocklike character needs to be seasoned with honeylike disposition.

I have seen persons hardened and embittered by suffering because they have not used it wisely. But I have seen many more who have been softened, mellowed and melted into Christlike personalities. They allowed suffering to be used as a chisel to smooth off the rough corners, as sandpaper to polish down the surface. They became tender, sympathetic, congenial and gracious. Eventually they were so tempered that they are able to smile through tears like an afternoon sun through an April shower. Their lives reflect the beauty of Christ like a sparkling dewdrop in the morning sun. They are resplendent with the brightness of Christ.

What a tragic loss of opportunity it is to waste our pains. When suffering is surrendered to Christ it can be used for something infinitely worthwhile.

Correction and Education

Third, people often wonder whether God imposes suffering as punishment for sin—that is, whether he punishes moral evil with utilitarian evil. I have already said that God does not make a general practice of imposing suffering arbitrarily for any purpose at all. I think we are safe in saying that he never does. Whether he allows the suffering to be used as punishment is another matter. If we believe that he does, we have to remember that it is only on rare occasions: we generally observe that suffering is experienced disproportionately to one's sins—the guilty suffering less than they deserve and the innocent often suffering more. So suffering does not necessarily point to the sin of the sufferer, and good health and wealth do not point to one's innocence.

Further, to allow suffering as punishment is more often than not totally unnecessary, because sooner or later moral evil has its own kickback on the one who commits the evil. Rather than saying that suffering is penalty for sin, it would be more accurate to say that suffering at times is the effect, the consequence, the automatic fallout of sin. The "punishment" is included in the scheme of things rather than being imposed directly on individuals.

If we allow the notion of retribution to include a corrective, educative element, I think we must admit that suffering is sometimes so used by God. But again the accent is on being used by God rather than imposed by God. Pain is used as God's broadcasting system. It is the only frequency to which some persons are tuned, the only wavelength from God they are willing to pick up. Out of mercy, not vengeance, God uses pain to awaken us to our moral poverty and need. Suffering has provided an occasion for countless numbers of persons to return to God.

Since pain can be corrective and educative, it sometimes provides an opportunity for self-evaluation. One can never really know how she or he would react to the severity of pain until one has the opportunity. The test of Christian commitment is found in a situation that sorts out one's real motives for commitment, a circumstance in which commitment is difficult to maintain. The test of one's motives in journeying through life with Christ comes when the pilgrimage is rough and steep, the road thorn fringed and storm swept. The test may reveal a better and stronger person than one expected to find. On the other hand it may shake us out of the illusion of our own goodness by showing us how cowardly, deceitful and morally weak we really are. We sometimes think of pain as God's test of whether we will remain true to him in times of difficulty. But he considers pain more an opportunity for us to test ourselves.

A Ministry of Suffering

Fourth, suffering is used by God to minister to other persons who have yet to traverse this frightening terrain. It is a ministry sometimes more effective than the most powerful sermon. To those of us who are not suffering, courage looks more courageous and virtue looks purer against a backdrop of affliction. The courage of such Christians as Helen Keller and Joni Eareckson has inspired millions of persons, not in spite of their affliction but precisely *because* of it.

On the island of Molokai in Hawaii, lepers were ministered to by loving attendants, but the attendants' strength to minister came from the courage of those to whom they ministered. Thus the suffering lepers ministered to the workers in a greater way than they themselves were ministered to. When Robert Louis Stevenson visited the island and saw the misery, he almost lost his faith in God. As he observed more closely, his faith returned. Before leaving he wrote in the hospital guest book the following lines:

To see the infinite pity of this place,
The mangled limb, the devastated face,
The innocent sufferer smiling at the rod—
A fool were tempted to deny his God.
He sees, he shrinks. But if he gaze again,
Lo, beauty springing from the breast of pain!

He marks the sisters on the mournful shores;
And even a fool is silent, and adores.

During my college days as a student pastor, a relatively young woman in the church lay on a hospital bed for several weeks dying a slow, malignant death. Long and exacting hours ground into days and weeks that seemed like centuries. Her physician told us that her pain was excruciating, not to mention the stress from indignities, loneliness and uncertainty. But from her personality there simply radiated the personality of Christ, until the air was crisp with divine Presence.

Late one Saturday afternoon after other visitors had left, she wept, putting to me that perplexing question that has puzzled humankind for many centuries. "Why, Pastor? Why doesn't God let me die? Why doesn't he let me out of this and get me off everybody else's hands? Why?" Perhaps it was a good thing I did not have an academic answer then. It would not have been much help at a time like that.

The next morning after my Sunday sermon I was greeting worshipers in the narthex as they filed out of the sanctuary. A young married couple whom I had never seen before stood aside until the others had left, then told me their story. When they had visited the hospital earlier in the week, Lucille Spencer had ministered to their souls. "We had never felt so close to Christ in our lives," the young man said. "We went home and decided that we want to become Christians." You can be sure that I made a beeline back to the hospital. This time I carried with me part of the answer.

Lucille had not realized at all that she had ministered to the couple. All she had done was to suffer and be true to Christ in her suffering. The hospital bed became a pulpit to communicate the life of God. And a young couple whom no minister had ever been able to reach for Christ went home and made a solemn vow. The suffering had become sacramental. It had not been in vain.

There is also quite another way that suffering can become a ministry. If I suffer, I minister to other persons by providing for them an occasion to minister to me. My suffering becomes an occasion for their sympathy. More than my need for sympathy is their need to be able to sympathize. While they minister to my lesser need I am ministering to their greater need. And here is a paradox: the more undeserved my suffering appears to be, the greater opportunity it provides for sympathy. So the more unmerited the suffering, the greater is the ministry of suffering.

Knowing God's Presence

Fifth, suffering is used by God as an opportunity for us to be able to sense and prize his divine presence. "What a Friend We Have in Jesus" was written by Joseph Scriven after his fiancée drowned. "O Love That Wilt Not Let Me Go" was written by George Matheson after his fiancée left him because it was discovered he was going blind. How many have found Christ as a real Person when they were flat on their backs and had no place to look but up? Many have caught that mysterious feeling that God was carrying their pain in his own heart. They have felt that intangible tap on the shoulder and heard in their souls that inaudible whisper, "Move over now. You forgot I'm in this with you. You are not alone."

An angry man says, "Where was your God when my mother lay suffering for months? Just where was your God then?" If he had asked his mother, the chances are she herself could have told him. God was right there at her bedside, suffering right along with her. Her pillow became his pillow. Her pain became his pain. Her sorrow was caught up in his own soul.

For more than seven years Air Force Colonel Robinson Risner was a prisoner of war in North Vietnam. At the time, few of us knew that our POWs were undergoing the torture they described after their return: isolation, deprivation, threats, the sheer physical torture of the "rope trick." Because of his military rank, Risner was subjected to more severe treatment and more solitary confinement than many of the others. But he said, "God was very close to me... I found a new relationship with God."[7]

Sometime ago I saw Colonel Risner on a television interview. After he had explained something of the unbearable torture, he looked straight into the eye of the camera and said, "I have tested God in ways many people will never be able to test him. And I can say that *I know*, even in a Hanoi prison camp, that God is *real*."[8]

God may become real to us through the beauty of a sunset, through the smile of a child, through the love of a friend. Some discover God through the springtime bursting with budding flowers, singing birds and growing grass. God becomes real to some in a splendid sanctuary with stained-glass windows, magnificent anthems and inspiring prayers. But to this man God became real in hunger, torture and isolation, in ridicule, rejection, filth and fear—in a prison camp on the other side of the world from home. God broke into that dark cell with a light brighter than cathedral chandeliers. And Robinson Risner could sing, "I know... that God is real."

Centuries earlier God said, "I will turn the darkness before them into light, ... and I will not forsake them" (Is 42:16).

14
VICTORY
OVER
SUFFERING

SOONER OR LATER FOR MOST persons the gate of suffering opens wide and beckons us to enter the world of pain. Our turn will have arrived. We enter fearfully, not recognizing it as a period of vast opportunity. Awaiting us are adventures of exploration that others cannot have. We learn things, see things and feel things never known by those who remain outside. We become a part of a royal company whose horizons have expanded, whose hearts have been tenderized and whose self-image has been enhanced. It is a land of honor and dignity with only one primary responsibility—to bear with regal bearing the problems of pain.

After all the intellectual explanations have been written and read, pain is still there to be experienced. The primary business of pain is not to be explained but to be borne.

Jesus did not explain the "why" of suffering—he endured it. He left it to the apostles and theologians to explain the cross. He bore it. And therein was his victory.

This chapter could better be written by hundreds of suffering individuals I have personally known. I am better at explaining pain than bearing it. They have borne it in their own lives with victory. Their feet have stood in thorns while their faces were bathed in light. They could write from experience. I am writing from observation of their experiences, from personal close-up observations of persons who have carried that light.

Earlier I said that the human constitution is constructed with a mechanism for tuning out or shutting off excessive pain. That same constitution is built to unleash additional courage and moral strength in times of pain. Most persons find themselves standing taller in pain than they ever stood before. Many gain a self-respect they never had before.

Explaining pain has to do with ideas but enduring pain has more to do with attitudes. Attitude is the one ingredient that spells out the difference between utility and futility, between victory and defeat, between rising above pain and collapsing under it. There are probably deep secrets of wholesome attitudes that I have never been aware of. The ones that follow are secrets I have observed in individuals who have suffered with dignity and grace.

Suffering Is Being Used
First, to know that one's suffering is being used for a worthwhile purpose promotes a healthy attitude. Something being used is not being wasted. Though suffering is not purposed, it is purposeful. It is not intended but it can be useful. The futility is overcome by significance.

Some of the purposes for which suffering can be used were listed in the previous chapter. What I consider to be the most important use of pain I have reserved until now to suggest. The least that can be said about pain is that it is disagreeable. Being so, it has the tendency to make one disagreeable to oneself. The pleasant things that have been lived for are replaced with pain. One's life becomes painful to live. With superficial sources of meaning lost, life is stripped of any false, artificial meanings that propped it up. There is a sense in which a suffering person loses his or her life—loses those things that made life worthwhile. Now one has a different life, which is dull, boring and painful.

To lose one's life in this way is like suicide—unless in losing superficial life one finds a genuine life. Suicide would mean that what is lost is not replaced by a greater gain. If some almost worthless values that gave an otherwise thin and empty life a tiny bit of substance are replaced with values that give life solidity and firmness, then that loss is the greatest thing that could happen. One's primary interest shifts from self to others and one's attitude is changed from simply getting to an attitude of giving. We lose our occupation with ourselves by being preoccupied with something bigger and beyond ourselves.

We cannot receive the real gifts of life until the playthings that we desperately cling to are wrenched from our grasp. Suffering may force us to lose a life that was not worth having in order to gain a life that will not be lost.

A paradoxical principle stated by Jesus has been proved a million times in the practical mathematics of life: "Whoever would save his life will lose it, and whoever loses his life for my sake will find it" (Mt 16:25). To lose oneself in Christ is to surrender a worthless life to gain a priceless one. That life and that quality of life even relatively few Christians know much about. A lot more suffering may be required before many of us can say with the apostle Paul, "But whatever gain I had, I counted as loss for the sake of Christ. Indeed I count everything as loss because of the surpassing worth of knowing Christ Jesus my Lord" (Phil 3:7-8).

That purpose *in* suffering leads to a purpose so far *beyond* suffering that at bedrock level the suffering is eclipsed. A purpose big enough to absorb the unanswerable contradictions inherent in suffering fits into a master program which will ultimately dissolve such contradictions without requiring an answer. We mortals need a program for living that is adequate to pull up the loose ends of life's frayed edges. If we have not yet zeroed in on that higher purpose to sustain us in our suffering, the suffering may have to be used for the very purpose of giving us a greater purpose in life than comfort, ease and health. Then we will know that what happens *in* us is infinitely more important than what happens *to* us. We can "hang loose" and roll with life's punches because we have found in Christ a life for ourselves that cannot be derailed or defeated by suffering. Nothing can break in on us that can destroy this bigger life.

Suffering Shared by God

A second secret of a victorious attitude is found in the Christian confidence that one's suffering is being shared by God himself. That removes our loneliness and sense of isolation. The pain we cannot find words to express is felt by God.

I have seen my children suffer ordinary childhood pains that I wished I could take into my body and bear for them. I could not do so because my body was not theirs, but at times my mental anguish over their pain has been more acute than their physical agony. Although as a spirit God cannot experience physical pain so far as we know, his mental anguish is greater than our physical. All human suffering is a dilution of the more substantive suffering of God. But the Christian faith teaches that God actually took on himself a physical body in Christ, experienced the unbearable suffering of a crucifixion and tasted death for every person. The prophet could write, "Surely he has borne our griefs and carried our sorrows. . . . He was wounded for our transgressions, he was bruised for our iniquities" (Is 53:4-5).

The words to the song "He Knows" put it this way:

He knows the bitter, weary way,
The endless strivings day by day;
The souls who weep, the souls that pray, . . .
He knows how hard the fight has been;
The clouds that come our souls between,
The wounds the world has never seen.
He knows when faint and worn we sink,
How deep the pain, how near the brink;
Of dark despair, we pause and shrink.
He knows! Oh, tho't so full of bliss,
For tho' our joys on earth we miss;
We still can bear it, feeling this,
He knows, He knows.

The Future Life

Third, the consciousness even in pain that we are ultimately in God's hands is reassuring. One of the messages in the Old Testament story of Job is that the outer boundary of our affliction is set by God. He said to Satan, "Take his wealth, his health, his friends and his own family, *but* . . ." There God drew the line: "Spare his life." Those who have shared life with Christ for many years feel secure in divine love, knowing that nothing can get through to them that is not first filtered through God's caring heart. God still stands guard over the universe. The intensity and duration of suffering has limits.

Fourth, the Christian faith emphasizes the importance of seeing the temporal in light of the eternal, the present in light of the future, temporary suffering from the standpoint of ultimate happiness.

Christians have been accused of a "dessert mentality" in anticipating heaven, of copping out to escape the emotional predicament of suffering by looking forward to future happiness. Of course, it *is* a kind of dessert mentality —doesn't a football team endure blocking and tackling while anticipating victory? It is copping out in the way a psychologist counsels a patient to think about the bright side of life rather than the dark. It is an escape in the same way that an expectant mother endures the inconveniences of pregnancy and the pains of childbirth by looking forward to the joys of motherhood. One rarely hears a mother mention the shadow of death she endured in order to become a mother.

Biblical glimpses into that life beyond do not portray persons going around complaining about the trials they suffered on earth. The general picture is that the memory of pain will fade into insignificance and even be forgotten by those who are filled with eternal joy. Paul said, "I consider that the sufferings of this present time are not worth comparing with the glory that is to be revealed to us" (Rom 8:18).

All life on earth is only a fleeting moment in the span of eternity. The sufferings here are little more than a passing dream in light of the reality of eternal joy. Moral good will prevail over utilitarian evil. Moral evil can never again sabotage utilitarian good. "Neither shall there be mourning nor crying nor pain any more, for the former things have passed away" (Rev 21:4).

This solution is often disparaged because it is to be found in a future world. But the anticipation of it is to be found in this world in the actual experience of suffering itself. It is in the next life that the problem of suffering will be solved. It is in anticipation of that solution that suffering can be borne.

Notes

[1]What I am calling the "problem" of good should not be understood as the counterpart or flip side of the problem of evil. The two problems do not have symmetrical derivations and should therefore be considered asymmetrical rather than symmetrical.

The problem of evil derives from the alleged incompatibility of the existence of evil with the existence of a good God, and is therefore a problem for the theist. The problem of good derives from the alleged incompatibility of the existence of good with the nonexistence of a good God and is consequently a problem for the nontheist. (In this preliminary chapter I am using *good* in its broader sense to include the aesthetic goodness of beauty in order and the utilitarian goodness of happiness as well as the goodness of moral values, all of which are recognized by many nontheists as "good.")

Up to this point the two problems are symmetrical. The symmetry breaks down in the *way* the propositions of each problem are incompatible. In the problem of evil for the theist, the existence of evil and the existence of a good God are thought to be deductively contradictory. (In chapter 3, I argue that the two propositions are not contradictory.) In the problem of good for the nontheist, however, the existence of good and the nonexistence of a good God are thought to be inductively improbable rather than deductively contradictory. The problem of evil results from alleged contradiction; the problem of good results from alleged improbabilities. One is deductive; the other is inductive.

What most Christians and non-Christians alike recognize as good in the world deserves an explanation for its existence. The serious student wants to know why such good abounds. Either there is a reason, or all is random. If the consistency, force and volume of the good we observe makes randomness improbable, then nontheists are under a burden to provide a reason. That is their problem. Theists have reason provided for them in the goodness of God, yet that raises for them the problem of evil—an alleged contradiction that I am contending can be resolved.

[2]Black, M., ed., *Philosophy in America* (London: Allen and Unwin, c. 1965), pp. 204-20.

[3]Mackie, J. L., "Evil and Omnipotence," in Basil Mitchell, ed., *The Philosophy of Religion* (London: Oxford University Press, 1971), p. 101.

[4]Those who insist that God should have created persons who would freely choose right have supposed that freedom of choice simply means a person has freedom to choose in a way that accords with the person's own nature or personality inclinations. The agent has freedom to be itself, to choose in a way that is consonant with itself, without being divinely constrained.

The contradiction arises when the nature is defined *as* the agent. To the agent has been ascribed freedom, but the nature of the person has been determined either by God or by outside forces. So we have freedom attributed to the agent and determinism attributed to the nature, while agent and nature are defined as one and the same. Thus to the same category or personality have been assigned two mutually exclusive predicates: freedom and determinism.

The agent itself, it seems to me, is something larger and more inclusive than character condition (nature). The agent is the person himself. The character condition is a predicate of the agent which is the subject. The agent then has another predicate (among many others) which I am calling the capacity or the *ability to perform an act*. The first predicate is locked inside a deterministic system, but the second predicate includes an element of freedom.

I am using the term *freedom* or the phrase *ability to perform an act* rather than the traditional phrase *free will* because "will" is often thought of as a faculty of human personality. This is an idea I am not contending for. The freedom I speak of is a precondition for action but not necessarily a faculty.

[5]The behaviorist attempts to show how what we call conscience is the product of conditioning from incentives of reward and threats of punishment. But without the embedded, often somewhat veiled notion of a principle of rightness, the incentives and threats could only condition a person to behave in a way to receive reward and avoid punishment. Some of us have yet to see how behavioristic conditioning alone can account for the feeling of guilt. The desire to comply with social norms may account for the feeling of shame from being "inferior" when one does not measure up. But the only way it can account for guilt, it seems to me, is for the social group itself to recognize a transcendent principle of rightness as a social norm. A particular guilt feeling may be partially explained by pointing to certain conditioning regarding what is right, but the fact of guilt feelings points beyond the conditioning to the notion that there is such a thing as rightness with which one ought to comply. Without the fixed notion that there is a right, the conditioning regarding what is right could never produce guilt.

[6]Quoted in Tryon Edwards, ed., *The New Dictionary of Thoughts* (New York: Standard Book Company, 1955), p. 171.

[7]Russell T. Hitt, "The POW Story," *The Herald*, 5 Sept. 1973, pp. 8-9, 13.

[8]Ford Philpot's TV show, "The Story," WLEX-TV, Lexington, Ky., 24 December 1973.